Managing an Organization

Managing an Organization

SECOND EDITION

Theodore Caplow

University of Virginia

Holt, Rinehart and Winston
New York • Chicago • San Francisco • Philadelphia
Montreal • Toronto • London • Sydney
Tokyo • Mexico City • Rio de Janeiro • Madrid

92833

Library of Congress Cataloging in Publication Data

Caplow, Theodore.
  Managing an organization.

  Rev. ed. of: How to run any organization. 1st ed.
c1976.
  Bibliography: p.
  Includes index.
  1. Management. 2. Organization. I. Title.
HD31.C343 1983   658.4   83-30

ISBN 0-03-058578-3 (General Book edition)

ISBN 0-03-059729-3 (College edition)

CBS COLLEGE PUBLISHING
Holt, Rinehart and Winston
The Dryden Press
Saunders College Publishing

Contents

Managing an Organization

Introduction

In authority, in power, in charge,
in control, in command,
at the head, at the helm,
at the wheel, in the saddle . . .
Excerpt from *Roget's Thesaurus*

Whom This Book Is For

This book is for any man or woman who is head of an organization. The organization may be as small as a racing crew or as large as a multinational corporation; the principles of management will be the same and the difficulties to be overcome will be similar.

Most books about management attempt to show executives and administrators at all levels how to perform their assignments efficiently and how to work effectively with superiors, equals, and subordinates. This book has nothing to say about working with superiors and equals; it assumes that you, the reader, are supreme in your domain. Even though the organization you lead may be part of a larger organization, this volume has nothing to say about getting along with capricious superiors and competitive colleagues. It is solely concerned with the challenging problem of how you can run your own organization so that your authority is secure, communications are good, the purposes of the organization are effectively fulfilled, the people in it want to stay, and changes in your organization's environment are successfully handled as they arise.

An earlier version of this book was called *How to Run Any Orga-*

1

nization, too cocky a title for so serious a book, but otherwise accurate. I know of at least two companies that require every department head to keep a copy of it in his or her desk. This new version covers the same ground with more emphasis on upward planning and other methods of inducing subordinates to lend you the full use of their brains. It is still a very thin book compared to textbooks on management-in-general, which run to 700 or 800 pages and are not designed for bedtime reading. They have to be heavy to take in the mass of practical detail involved in such subjects as budgetary planning, personnel administration, and marketing and other matters that white-collar workers in large companies need to know about.

The present book is thinner because the basic principles of managing an organization successfully happen to be rather simple and straightforward. These principles, which have to do with the coordination of other people's efforts, do not vary appreciably from one type of organization to another or even, I would insist, from one culture to another. The right way to run an organization is the same in Patagonia and in Minnesota, whatever the differences in appearance.

The theory of managing an organization is much easier to understand than it is to follow in daily practice. Perfect managers are as rare as perfect wives or perfect ballplayers. Good managers, however, are not uncommon. For the most part they are made, not born, and the easiest way to become a good manager is to understand the theory, apply it in the real world, learn from mistakes, and learn even more from the experience of doing things right.

What an Organization Is

An organization is a social system deliberately established to carry out some definite purpose. It consists of a number of people in a pattern of relationships. The pattern is not entirely dependent on the particular persons who belong to the organization at a given time. The organization assigns a *position* to each of its members, and the incumbent of a position has a set part to play in the organization's collective *program.* Every organization has a program—a set of planned activities that can go well or badly. If they consistently go well, the organization thrives. If they go badly, it disappears or is restructured for another try. The manager of an organization is the person who has the primary responsibility for making its activities go well.

An organizational program always involves considerably more than one central activity. Whether the central activity is a production process, a game, a fight, or a ceremony, the organization must also maintain its internal structure, keep its members happy, and adapt to changes in the external environment. In addition, the manager of any organization has the peculiar and personal problem of establishing authority. In discussing problems, we will take that one up first, since unless the manager can keep the right to manage, the other parts of the managerial assignment quickly become irrelevant. The first chapter of this manual is about "Authority."

It does the organization little good, however, for the manager to establish authority unless that authority is used to hold the organization together and achieve its purposes. Holding the organization together does not imply that all members of the organization will have identical goals and agree about how to achieve them, but it does require them to agree sufficiently for the organization to pursue its collective goals in a unified way. This limited agreement results from continuous communication up, down, and sideways within the organization. Most of this communication flows through established channels, formal or informal, and is modified in predictable ways by these channels. All this is discussed in the second chapter, "Communication."

But communication is not an end in itself. It is a means of getting the organization's job done, which is, of course, what management is all about. A manager is someone who supervises the work of others and can, by his or her own actions, increase or diminish their productivity. In practice, there are two quite different modes of supervision—direct and indirect—and they call for somewhat different strategies. In addition to the problems of routine supervision, there are all sorts of special problems that appear in any division of labor and interfere with the efficiency or the effectiveness of a work group. These matters are considered in chapter three, "Productivity."

The belief that productivity and morale are necessarily correlated is part of the folklore of organization. Like most folklore, it contains a grain of truth. Sudden increases in productivity are likely to stimulate short-term improvements of morale, and vice versa. But the general relationship between productivity and morale is more complex. As empirical studies in diverse types of organization have shown, high morale often accompanies low productivity, and crises of morale may be brought about by rising productivity. There is always some significant relationship between the output of an organization and the emotions of its members, but the relationship is far too intricate to suggest that productivity and morale are interchangeable. The managerial policies that sustain morale are described in "Morale," the fourth chapter.

No organization, however limited its goals, can safely ignore the larger social systems from which it draws its people and its resources. Every organization attempts to control the external environment, but no matter how large, rich, or sacred it becomes, it cannot develop any real immunity to changes in the external environment. Some of these external changes are attributable to the organization's own activities; some result from long-term trends and can be anticipated in a general way; some are so surprising that they cannot be imagined until they have actually occurred. In a complex, modern society, this last category is nearly inexhaustible. The unanticipated effects of legislation, technology, political upheavals, moral fashions, migration and other forms of mobility; innovations in transportation, communication, and entertainment; the movement of prices, and the fluctuation of scarcities now guarantee a fairly adventurous history to even the most insulated and reclusive organizations, such as craft unions and boarding schools. The problem of adapting an organization to external change is particularly challenging because external changes not only affect the conditions under which the organization pursues its goals but may also transform the goals. The problems that arise in this way cannot be as neatly resolved as some of those discussed under other headings, but they are not hopelessly difficult, as we shall see in the final chapter, "Change."

These five topics—authority, communication, productivity, morale, and change—are the substance of this manual. We shall take them up in order, but before turning to the first topic I would like to draw your attention to some basic principles of management.

Basic Principles of Management

1. All human organizations resemble each other so closely that much of what is learned by managing one organization can be applied to managing any other organization. Every organization, for example, has a collective identity; a roster of members, friends, and antagonists; a program of activity and a time schedule to go with it; a table of organization; a set of formal rules partly contradicted by informal rules; procedures for adding and removing members; utilitarian objects used for organizational tasks; symbolic objects used in organizational rituals; a history; a special vocabulary; some elements of

folklore; a territory; and a method of placing members within that territory according to their relative importance. Every organization has a division of labor that allocates specialized tasks to its members and a status order that awards them unequal shares of authority, honor, and influence.

2. Every organization—except the very smallest—is a cluster of suborganizations of varying sizes, which are organizations in their own right and have all of the features described above. Some suborganizations are departments of the parent organization; some are illegitimate factions of it; some are formally independent of it, like a union local in a factory, or attached to it temporarily, like an orchestra hired for a club dance. The important thing to remember about suborganizations is that their goals are never completely compatible with the goals of the parent organization. It is seldom possible to reform a suborganization for the benefit of the parent organization without encountering resistance. On the other hand, it is quite impossible to manage a large organization without occasionally offending, damaging, or destroying some of its suborganizations.

3. The problems of managing a large organization are similar to the problems of managing a small or medium-sized organization, if only because every large organization is run by a managerial oligarchy which is itself a small organization—there is no other way to do it. Problems of communication, data retrieval, and public relations are necessarily more complex in a large organization, but there are more people to help with them too. Running a large organization should not require more of your time and effort than running a small organization. If it does, something is probably wrong with the way your job is set up or with your personal style.

4. During any given interval in an organization's history, it will be growing, stable, or declining. Some organizations, such as business corporations, normally strive for growth but do not always achieve it. Some, such as exclusive clubs, attempt to avoid either growth or decline. Others, such as legislatures and baseball teams, have a fixed number of members, although the number of assistants and supernumeraries can vary. Still others, such as social movements past their peak, continue to operate for long periods of time while declining in size. The task of management is easiest in a growing organization because growth itself—whatever its real cause—is usually viewed as a sign of managerial success and because the input of new resources occasioned by growth can be used to pay for mistakes. Managing a stable organization is a more difficult task and calls for

a finer adjustment of means and ends, careful decision-making, and alertness to the external environment. The management of a declining organization may be easy or hard, depending upon whether the decline is regarded as inevitable. In the face of an inevitable decline, standards of managerial performance may be low. In the case of a decline that is regarded as reversible, the task of the manager is always difficult and sometimes impossible.

5. Most organizations find it harder to satisfy one of their goals than others, for reasons beyond their control. When this is the case, the manager's success with the critical goal is the thing that matters, while the achievement of other goals is overlooked or taken for granted. Maintaining authority is critical, for example, in a prison or penitentiary; maintaining membership is what counts in a civic association; as director of a summer camp you are judged almost exclusively by whether you can keep up morale; as coach of a football team that can win all its games you need not worry about much else.[1] Thus, every type of organization tends to develop managers who are overspecialized in the accomplishment of one assignment and who minimize their other responsibilities until this neglect catches up with them in the shape of rebellion, schism, bankruptcy, or reform by outsiders.

6. Many organizations develop crises from time to time. An organizational crisis is a situation in which the priorities of management are forcibly rearranged by some unforeseen combination of circumstances. The qualities that you, as manager, are called upon to display in a crisis may be quite different from those routinely required. College presidents are called on for personal courage, prison wardens are asked to show Christian charity, long-term planners are compelled to make snap decisions. Skill and luck play equal parts in the management of crisis. The skill can be practiced, but not the luck, so that while a few well-handled major crises may strengthen an organization and its leadership, a long series of crises will almost certainly ruin it. If you, as a manager, perceive your role as "putting out fires," then you are a poor manager and ought to be replaced by someone who attaches more importance to fire prevention. The fundamental procedures for preventing organizational crises are early detection and the rehearsal of drills that transform crises into routine problems.

CHAPTER ONE

Authority

There was trouble in the State of Lu,
and the reigning monarch called
on Confucius to ask for his help;
when the Master arrived at the court,
he went to a public place and took a seat
in the correct way, facing south,
and all trouble disappeared.

From a Chinese chronicle

Love, Fear, and Charisma

Opinions differ about whether it is better for a manager to be loved or feared by subordinates, but to be loved *and* feared is best of all.[1]

Fear is a normal reaction to anyone who embodies uncontrollable power over oneself, who can reward and punish without restraint. The courtiers of Henry VIII or the Grand Turk lived in a constant exhilaration of fear, knowing that the master with whom they associated daily could end their lives with a casual word. I have seen lieutenants paralyzed by the appearance of a brigadier general and professors backing away from a university president with profound bows. I knew a chef so feared in his kitchen that the cooks' knees knocked visibly at his approach. It is not at all unusual for foremen and choirmasters to arouse panic in their groups, not to mention the Mafia dons and high school principals whose stock in trade is their ability to scare people.

Love is another spontaneous reaction to authority. The love of armies for their generals has been one of history's strongest forces. There is always some love between a good teacher and a good class, and even between good chairmen and their committees. Many a

7

modern executive would leave spouse and child, parent and friend, to follow a boss.

The talent for arousing fear and love in followers is called *charisma*. The term was invented by the great German sociologist Max Weber to describe a type of nonbureaucratic leadership, but charisma is abundantly displayed in bureaucratic organizations, too. We tend to think of it as a kind of natural gift, like musical talent, but the empirical evidence does not support this view. In some positions, such as the speakership of a legislature, nearly every incumbent appears charismatic; in other instances, it seems to be the combination of a particular personality and a particular position that generates charisma. A few of history's most charismatic figures—Mary Baker Eddy and Pope John XXIII come to mind—developed their charisma in old age. There is no single constellation of personality traits we can associate with charisma. Some charismatic figures are marked by their enthusiastic vitality, others by their pale austerity; some are sociable, others withdrawn; some use their power to win lovers, others avoid all intimate contacts. If we look at the most charismatic figures of a particular era, it is hard to discern any common traits they have except intelligence and energy. What other resemblances can be found between Abraham Lincoln and John F. Kennedy, between Hitler and Chairman Mao, between Mahatma Gandhi and Indira Gandhi?

But to return to management on a more modest scale, how is one to be both feared and loved by some (never all) of one's followers? What makes a manager feared is the reputation of acting ruthlessly when the interests of the organization, as he or she conceives them, are opposed to the interests of individuals. The establishment of such a reputation is partly a matter of style and partly a matter of substance. The appropriate style is to impose punishment promptly and confidently, without any interest in the excuses of the offender. One or two harsh actions of this kind can make a leader more feared than a whole reign of terror conducted in a more capricious manner.

The best policy to follow in developing a reputation for severity is to make any decision that involves a conflict between the organization and an individual according to fixed principles announced in advance and applied so consistently that each application takes on a didactic character. Nearly every organization, for example, must eventually deal with a theft of organizational property by a member. The offense cannot be ignored without inviting trouble. It does not matter so much whether the punishment is prosecution or expulsion or demotion or counseling, but it does matter that the full penalty be invoked in every case without much regard to extenuating circumstances or to the possibility of reprisal by the offender's friends.

Organizational love is even more predictable than organizational fear. For you to be loved as a manager, your organization's program must be successful, its success must be attributable to you, and you must develop a reputation for acts of kindness to individual followers. Success is the essential element in this formula. Without it, an organization will not love its leader at all, although after conspicuous success has aroused devotion to a leader, the attachment sometimes persists throughout a subsequent period of failure. More often it does not. Football coaches and political candidates who win consistently are loved despite bad habits and defective characters. The greater the organization's success, the easier it is for the leader to claim the credit and the less likely it is that the claim will be disputed. If your organization is extremely successful—your football team undefeated or your party swept into office by a landslide—it may not even be necessary for you, the leader, to perform those small acts of kindness toward individuals which assure the onlookers of your potential goodwill toward themselves. If you are genuinely kind and sympathetic, so much the better; a whole body of anecdote and legend will grow up around you. If you are not, the myth of your kindness will spring up by itself or will be fabricated. Organizational success is the vital ingredient in the love potion.

We are getting a little ahead of our story. Before you, as a manager, can be feared or loved for your achievements, you must first assume your office, discover its powers and limitations, and actually exercise the authority to which you are entitled in theory. This process always takes some time and causes some trouble. Let us look at it more closely.

Assuming the Office

Leaving out those few managers who obtain an office by founding a new organization, most new managers are installed as successors to a former manager. They key elements in succession are the strength of the predecessor and where the successor comes from.[2] Four basic situations are outlined in the table below: an outsider who follows a strong predecessor, an insider who follows a strong predecessor, an outsider who follows a weak predecessor, and an insider who follows a weak predecessor.

The most promising of these situations is that of the outsider who follows a weak predecessor. In that case, the new incumbent is sure of a welcome but is not bound by the predecessor's policy or constrained either to imitate or to avoid the predecessor's style. The least promising situation is that of an insider who follows a strong predecessor. If you imitate the predecessor's style you will appear inadequate or ludicrous to those who knew you in a subordinate capacity, while if you change the style and modify the policies that have been working so well, you will seem foolish and perhaps disloyal. There is no easy way out of this trap. In the long history of hereditary monarchy, very few sons of highly successful fathers were successful in turn, except when the son was allowed to assume his duties gradually—before the father's disappearance from the scene. Philip II of Spain was thus introduced to power by Charles V and Marcus Aurelius by the Emperor Hadrian, two of the rare instances when a great ruler was able to transfer power to an heir without loss of momentum. This solution requires more foresight, good judgment, and generosity on the part of the predecessor than is often to be found. Donald B. Trow's study of executive succession in more than a hundred manufacturing companies found that in a stable, family-owned company in which the manager's son was the potential successor, he was usually regarded as unfit for the job.[3] Without special preparation, the inside successor's best hope is to promise to imitate his great predecessor and then to involve the organization in a conflict, a merger, or some other adventure large enough to change its character.

As an insider following a weak predecessor, you may do fairly well if you are the leader of a rebellious faction that overthrew the old regime and if, upon taking office, you treat the adherents of the old regime decisively, removing them or winning them over, as circumstances allow. Unless you can do one or the other, your term of office will be short and unhappy. An insider succeeding a weak predecessor to whom loyalty is owed is in so hopeless a situation that only luck can solve the problem.

The most interesting of the four situations is that of an outsider who follows a strong predecessor. This can work out well or badly, and the outcome is largely determined by the new incumbent. If this is your case, then you should try to develop a personal style that contrasts sharply with the style of your predecessor while retaining most of the policies that have made the organization strong. If your predecessor was a frosty autocrat, you can be friendly and outgoing. If bu-

Chances of Success in
Various Types of Managerial Succession

	Strong Predecessor	Weak Predecessor
Inside successor	Chances unfavorable	Chances uncertain
Outside successor	Chances moderately favorable	Chances very favorable

reaucratic procedures have been previously emphasized, your new style may encourage informality. If the former policies emphasized growth, your new watchword might be stability. If your predecessor had a strong personal staff, it can be dismantled; if he or she worked alone, the time is ripe to recruit assistants. Such actions, baldly described, seem whimsical, but they work in real life, as shown by such excellent case studies of succession as Alvin Gouldner's *Patterns of Industrial Bureaucracy*[4] and Robert H. Guest's *Organizational Change*.[5] The rationale for a dramatic change of style is partly psychological and partly structural. Psychologically, you, as the successor, cannot hope to escape unfavorable comparison with your successful predecessor unless you appear to be so different as to make comparison difficult. Structurally, you cannot hope to take over the hierarchy of support that sustained the authority of your predecessor. In order to gain control of the organization, you have to restructure the existing hierarchy and change the distribution of authority and influence in your own favor. You cannot do this by shifting people around on a large scale. You probably lack authority to do so, and even if you have it, you cannot distinguish your potential friends from your potential foes at so early a stage. The existing hierarchy can be more tactfully, and just as effectively, reorganized by modifying a few key goals. If the prison's purpose is shifted from custody to rehabilitation, or the firm's primary interest from sales volume to profitability, or the college moves from selective to open admissions, the key figures of the old regime will inevitably lose influence and be supplanted by people more beholden to the new regime. The danger in this strategy is that the former group may perceive the threat and organize a mutiny. Whether such a mutiny is actually attempted and whether it succeeds in overturning the new regime is largely, although not entirely, determined by the timing of the new manager's actions, the topic to which we turn next.

The Honeymoon Period

Nearly every inauguration, from that of a pope or a president down to that of a restaurant manager or a platoon sergeant, is followed by a honeymoon period during which the new incumbent is almost exempt from criticism and his authority is almost unresisted.* It can be used either to ratify the existing organizational structure or to introduce sweeping changes, but it cannot be used for both purposes at once. As the new manager you must make this choice very early. You need not announce your choice, but not to make it is a serious error.

To make no innovations at all and to carry on exactly in your predecessor's style is a practicable policy if you are an insider who is following a strong predecessor by whom you were trained and sponsored. In the three other situations, the decision to leave well enough alone is highly questionable. The strategy new managers most often choose is to lie low during the honeymoon, using the respite to arrange furniture and files, choose assistants, study the organization, and meet the people who matter. The theory behind this strategy is that all serious decisions should be deferred until you, as the new incumbent, have enough information to foresee the consequences of any change you make and enough contacts to provide good feedback. The great defect of this strategy is that it wastes the unique opportunity offered by the honeymoon to make major innovations without arousing major resistance.

The strategy of lying low during the honeymoon is appropriate for an outsider following a weak predecessor. If such is the case, your situation is so favorable that you need not hurry to establish your control of the organization, while at the same time you have an acute need for information.

The same strategy is clearly advantageous for the insider following a strong predecessor. If you enter office with the direct sponsorship

---

*The honeymoon metaphor goes back to Thomas Jefferson, who, contemplating the prospect of being elected President, wrote to a friend in 1796 that "the honey moon would be as short in that case as in any other, and its moments of extasy would be ransomed by years of torment. . . ."

of your predecessor, any changes in style or policy that you introduced early in your term of office will be seen as a kind of disloyalty. If you take office on your own, your initial authority will not be sufficient to innovate safely, and any innovation you attempt may become the occasion of a humiliating setback. Your best hope is to lie low, cultivate friends and supporters, and wait for changes in the organizational climate.

The alternative strategy is to use the protection provided by the honeymoon to introduce sweeping changes, including dismissals and reassignments of personnel. This appears to be the optimum strategy for both the outsider who follows a strong predecessor and the insider who follows a weak one, although for somewhat different reasons. The outsider who follows a strong predecessor must establish authority at once or else may never be able to do so. The immunity offered by the honeymoon gives you a chance to demonstrate authority by introducing major changes before the old guard has a chance to begin the mutiny it will inevitably attempt. The only thing that limits your role as a new broom sweeping clean is your ignorance of the organization and the danger that some of your innovations will have disastrous results. You can protect yourself against this danger by emphasizing changes of style and general policy and avoiding projects that require detailed implementation. Your reign of terror ought to be highly selective and limited to a small number of potential opponents. The other key figures in the organization, having been edified by these examples, should be encouraged and supported in every possible way.

If you are an insider following a weak predecessor you should follow a similar policy during the honeymoon except that, since your position is shakier and your authority more questionable at the beginning, your program of innovation should be as comprehensive as the circumstances allow and should emphasize changes of policy over changes of style. A selective reign of terror is inadvisable for someone already involved in the organization's network of friendships and antagonisms. Either you must attempt to remove all your potential opponents, which will ruin you in nine cases out of ten, or you must try to win them over by forgiving and forgetting past differences. This policy, too, will often be ruinous; but any insider following a weak predecessor is slated for trouble anyway, and the odds, such as they are, favor a conciliatory approach. This table summaries the foregoing advice:

Recommended Honeymoon Strategies for New Managers

	Strong Predecessor	Weak Predecessor
Inside successor	Lie low	New broom, emphasizing changes of policy
Outside successor	New broom, emphasizing changes of style	Lie low

Finding the Purse Strings

So critical is the honeymoon for a new manager that by the time it ends, either by the accumulation of petty issues or the eruption of a major crisis, your eventual success or failure may be already assured. It is much easier for you to guarantee failure by your own actions than to guarantee success, which is subject to factors outside your control. Your eventual downfall as a manager is predictable if you have not secured control of the organization's finances by the end of the honeymoon. The power of the purse is the fundamental prerogative of management—in a government or in a glee club. As a newly inaugurated leader who expects to be preoccupied by statesmanship or polyphony you may be shocked to discover that money has become your principal concern and will remain so as long as you remain in charge. It is possible that you rose to office by displaying other abilities, and that you regard finance as the grubby business of bookkeepers and accountants; but you had better recognize that money is what management is mostly about and train yourself quickly to your new trade. There is no way of managing an organization successfully without exerting effective control over its expenditures. Practically speaking, this means that you, as the new manager of an organization, must study its accounts until you know all about the sources of its funds, how they are kept, how disbursements are authorized and audited, and how much authority you have with respect to each type of transaction. This course of study may be full of sad surprises, either because the organization is less solvent than it appears, or because fiscal control has drifted into other hands and cannot easily be recovered, or because a pattern of fixed expenses inherited from the past or imposed by outsiders limits the scope of managerial action. The unpleasantries, whatever they are, need to be learned, absorbed, and built into the framework of decision-making. Usually, when you have done your homework and learned the location of the purse strings you will have to engage in several sharp scuffles to gain possession of them. How to keep them in possession, once secured, is a problem that requires close attention to the table of organization.

Tables of Organization

A table of organization is a chart that shows all the positions in an organization and the relationships of authority and responsibility by which they are connected. The trick of describing an organization by such a chart, with its little boxes connected by vertical and horizontal lines, is relatively modern—the earliest known example comes from around 1900—but the underlying idea is as old as the pyramids. Nearly every serious discussion of an organization, including the discussion a new manager has with friends or sponsors before accepting the job, starts by laying out the table of organization. The table of organization does not tell us everything there is to know about the organizational structure, but no one seriously expects it to do so. Among the omitted details are most of the relationships between people who have no authority or responsibility with respect to each other, but must coordinate their activities anyway. Also omitted—by definition—are the informal norms which, in every organization, concentrate more authority in certain positions than the table of organization anticipates; and all the personal preferences, alliances and coalitions, exchanges of favors, interferences by outsiders, and customary breaches of the rules that develop in every organization.

What the table of organization *does* include, however, cannot be ignored by a manager without inviting immediate trouble. Nearly every table of organization has distinctive peculiarities not shared by organizations of other types, or even by other organizations of the same type. Being a sort of social machine, it has in most cases been deliberately designed for its functions. Like any other machine, it may be well or badly designed, cumbersome or streamlined, wasteful or economical, modern or antiquated. From the manager's standpoint, a good table of organization is one that makes the job easy, and a bad table of organization is one that makes it difficult. Since you are preoccupied with gaining authority upon taking office, your first review of the table of organization will probably focus on the question of how much authority you are allowed.

The proper design of tables of organization is the most controversial topic in modern management theory. A fine summary of the principal issues can be found in Learned and Sproat's *Organization Theory and Policy*.[6] The principal points on which experts disagree are: (a) the relative advantages of centralized and decentralized authority; (b) the desirability of unity of command ("one man, one boss") as compared to functional supervision; (c) whether any independent authority should be exercised by staff personnel; (d) the relative advantages of directive and participative decision-making. Some of these issues are more apparent than real. Nearly all serious students in this field now agree that there is no single form of pyramid or style of leadership that fits all organizations but that, on the contrary, the functions performed by a given organization must be taken into account to determine whether it will run better on a centralized or decentralized basis, and under authoritarian or democratic leadership. Furthermore, many poorly run organizations need more centralization *and* more decentralization, more direction *and* more participation, all at the same time.

In the discussion that follows, we will consider the table of organization from the special standpoint of the new manager engaged in establishing authority. The first necessity is access to all parts of the organization. The worst possible arrangement is that in which all contact between manager and organization is monitored by a powerful gatekeeper who can manipulate the flow of information upward and downward. Some marvelously inept managers, like Richard Nixon and Ferdinand VII of Spain, have installed such arrangements on their own initiative. More commonly, a new manager inherits such an arrangement after it has grown up under a weak or careless predecessor. When the outsider appointed to the presidency of the company described in Figure 1 discovers that the comptroller, the general counsel, the research director, and the heads of major operating departments all report to the executive vice-president, he knows that he has only a fighting chance of establishing his authority. In a small organization like a retail store, an elementary school, or a social agency, the manager needs direct contact with, and some control over, every member of the organization. In a large organization, direct contact is not feasible, but it should still be possible for the manager to initiate direct communication anywhere in the organization and to punish or reward any individual in it. If these re-

Figure 1. A Poor Table of Organization, from the New President's Standpoint

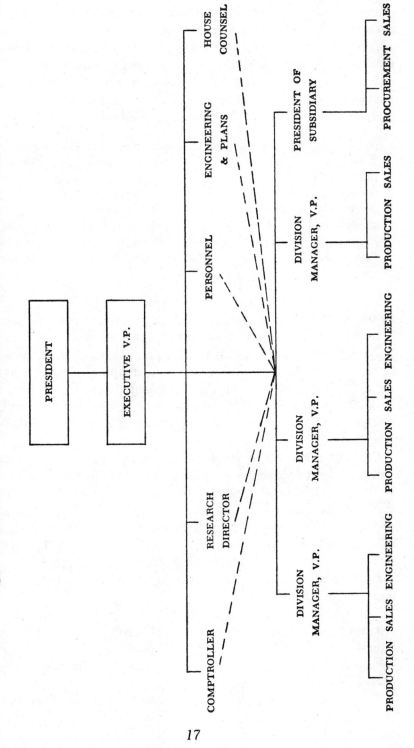

quirements are not met, the organization is partly out of control, but a degree of manageability can be salvaged, if the manager must approve all appointments, promotions, and transfers. When even this limited prerogative is lacking, as in the factories of the French tobacco monopoly described by Michel Crozier in *The Bureaucratic Phenomenon,* the manager becomes a figurehead with hardly any influence on the enterprise over which he presides.

> . . . The director's role in the plant is small. Production goals are narrowly fixed by the central office. Processes are stable and change is extremely difficult. The director does not have the right either to hire or to fire; he does not even have the right to assign workers to various jobs. The only people who are really dependent on him are those in the extremely weak supervisors' group. His only chance of making his influence felt is to administer the rules in such a way as to diminish the constant squabbling their application brings, and, in that way, to inspire people with more positive attitudes toward production.[7]

Only the fact that his own job is so secure as to be scarcely affected by his own performance makes it possible for the director of such an establishment to continue in office with some equanimity.

From the manager's standpoint, the people below him in the table of organization can be divided into four groups; (1) personal assistants, (2) headquarters staff, (3) subordinate managers, and (4) the rank-and-file. It may help in visualizing the relationship of these four categories if we point out who they are in organizations of different types.

Consider the company president shown in Figure 2. His personal assistants include an office manager, three secretaries, two assistants to the president, a receptionist, and a chauffeur; his headquarters staff are the company comptroller, the heads of the legal, personnel, and public relations departments, and the vice-presidents in charge of research and development, marketing and production. The subordinate managers shown in the table are group vice-presidents and presidents of subsidiaries. Lower managers and the rank-and-file are omitted from the table.

Now consider a neighborhood church. The minister's personal assistants are his part-time secretary and his wife; the sexton and the organist are his headquarters staff; the choirmaster and the Sunday school superintendent are subordinate managers. The congregation makes up the rank-and-file.

In tiny organizations, two of these roles may be combined in the

Figure 2. A Good Table of Organization, from the New President's Standpoint

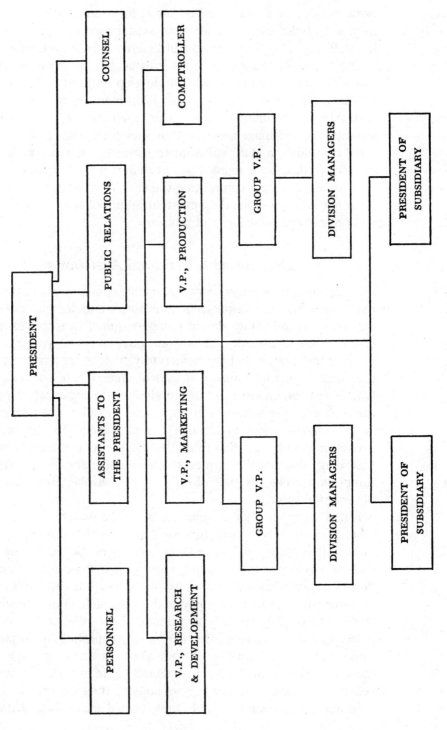

same person. In a road-mending crew, for example, the timekeeper may be both the foreman's personal assistant and the sole member of his staff, but he will be treated a little differently in each role.

The larger the organization, the greater the number of successive layers of management are likely to develop until, in a very large organization like the United States government, most of the people with whom the chief executive deals, even among his personal assistants, have management structures of their own, including personal assistants, a staff, subordinate managers, and a rank-and-file. But this complexity is more apparent than real since, from the standpoint of any manager confronting the table of organization for which he or she is responsible, the same four groups of subordinates appear and present the same kinds of problems.

Dealing with Personal Assistants

As you, the new manager, review the table of organization, you must make sure that all your personal assistants are under your direct and exclusive control. They should not be required to report to anyone else or even to consult with anyone else except at your direction. Each of them ought to be beholden to you alone for pay and promotion, and subject to dismissal at your discretion. A personal assistant who is too responsive to someone else in the organization poses a threat to even the strongest manager and should not be tolerated for longer than it takes to arrange a replacement. In the medieval French monarchy, the first thing that happened at the accession of a new king was that the former king's chamberlain came before the throne and broke his staff of office. By a sensible custom, he was never reappointed.

If it is important that personal assistants be under no obligation to other persons, it is equally important that they not acquire authority over staff officials and subordinate managers. Because they enjoy daily access to you, the manager, know your secrets, and control your flow of information, personal assistants who are faithful and competent inevitably acquire more power than the table of organization assigns to them. It is one of your principal responsibilities to keep this power in constant check. This can be accomplished by keeping the rank, pay, and perquisites of your personal assistants well below those of other people in the managerial circle and by constant surveillance to make sure they are not abusing their informal authority.

In absolute monarchies and family-owned businesses, if the man or woman responsible for management lacks talent or inclination for the job, they may delegate their power to a personal assistant—a mistress or favorite like Pompadour or Buckingham; a private secretary like Wolsey or Richelieu; a bodyguard like Henry Ford's Harry Bennett. The theory behind the rule of personal assistants is that since the power they exercise is illegitimate and universally resented, they remain totally dependent on their patrons and can be dismissed without any trouble whenever the patron's enthusiasm cools. The experiment has been tried innumerable times with varied outcomes, but that story would take us too far afield. In the long run, the practice of ruling through a personal assistant seems to lead either to a revolution that overthrows the regime or to a new constitution in which the head of the organization becomes a ceremonial figure and the assistant, as shogun or grand vizier, becomes the legitimate manager.

Dealing with the Headquarters Staff

The most interesting part of a table of organization, from the manager's standpoint, is the section of it close to the top where the responsibilities of the headquarters staff are shown. Your relationships with these key people are usually troublesome, since you are naturally dependent on them for information and advice but their individual interests differ from your own. Each of the key staff people is the advocate of a specialized approach to the organization's problems, for which they want more scope than their colleagues are willing to concede. Each of them is additionally responsible for giving information and advice to subordinate managers, which involves them in permanent conflicts with other staff officials and a potential conflict with you. At this level of the organization, more than at any other, the conflicting principles that enter into organizational decisions seem to be embodied in live protagonists: Mr. Skinflint the comptroller, Mr. Shakefinger the lawyer, Mr. Spellbinder the marketing executive, Dr. Testube the research director, all with axes to grind.

A good table of organization includes certain specific provisions about the staff:

First, the major staff officials ought to be clearly unequal in rank, pay, influence, and other status attributes, since if two or more of them are nearly equal, their struggles for predominance will keep the organization in a constant state of turmoil.

Second, they ought to meet frequently with the manager as a council or cabinet so that most of their disputes can be resolved by direct interaction or by the persuasion of a majority opinion. If they meet frequently without the manager, they will probably come to perceive him or her as their common enemy. If they do not meet at all, they will use the manager as the rope in their tugs-of-war. In council, the manager's role as chairman makes it possible to encourage a coalition against any malcontent without losing the benefit of the malcontent's advice, as in the famous case of President Lincoln and Secretary Stanton.

Third, the relationships between staff officials and the subordinate managers should be somewhat ambiguous. On the one hand, the organization cannot control subordinate managers if they are not fully responsive to line authority. On the other hand, even the most decentralized organization requires its departments to conform to certain fixed procedures, and these generally fall within the jurisdiction of the staff. The desirable ambiguity in the staff-line relationship whereby each party considers itself superior but fears to push the claim too far is secured by a number of conventional devices. Staff officials should be approximately equal in rank and perquisites to the subordinate managers with whom they deal; or perhaps a little lower to make up for the informal perquisites they acquire by proximity to the central authority. The people who carry out staff functions for a subordinate manager should report information to, and receive directives from, the headquarters staff but remain dependent on the subordinate manager for pay and promotion. A subordinate manager should never be required to go through the staff to obtain access to the manager, nor should the manager allow the direct channels of communication to the line to be blocked by staff officials.

Provisions for ambiguity invariably generate some friction between staff and line, but the definite predominance of one party or the other has graver consequences. When the staff is clearly on top, as in many social agencies, managers become grossly inefficient in their efforts to satisfy incompatible demands. When the line clearly dominates the staff, as in some research institutes, the organization develops a remarkable capacity to nullify managerial decisions.

Dealing with Subordinate Managers

Subordinate managers need to be treated differently from staff officials, so differently that the rules a manager ought to follow are almost—but not quite—reversed when turning from one group to the other. The constant objective in dealing with staff officials is to keep them from assuming too much responsibility. The constant objective in dealing with subordinate managers is to encourage them to assume as much responsibility as possible. The empirical evidence for this prescription is set forth at length in such books as Rensis Likert's *New Patterns of Management*[8] and Georges Friedmann's *Le Travail en Miettes*.[9] The unifying theme in these works is that the morale and productivity of an operating department can often be improved by giving it more independent responsibility for its part of the organization program. When subordinates are given more autonomy, their emotional commitment to the organizational program often increases in a dramatic way. On the technical side, their familiarity with operational details often enables them to run a given operation more effectively within broad guidelines than under tight instructions. One paradoxical result is that the manager who gives the fullest possible autonomy to subordinates may find his power over them enhanced rather than diminished, because evaluation of their performance becomes vastly more important to them as their responsibility for that performance increases. This procedure can be carried down through successive levels of the hierarchy to the individual worker, considered as the smallest possible "operating department." On each level, the transfer of decision-making power from the superior to the subordinate increases the subordinate's commitment to his tasks and reinforces, rather than diminishes, the authority of the superior.

The secret that under certain conditions the more authority a manager gives away, the more is left, was discovered by Elton Mayo and his associates in "human relations research" about half a century ago.[10] It was the second critical event in the history of scientific management; the first was the invention of time-and-motion analysis by Frederick Taylor a generation earlier. The Mayo discovery has given rise to innumerable innovations in the management of large-scale organizations under such labels as group dynamics, federal decentralization, conference methods, job enlargement, sensitivity training, and participatory democracy. In some experiments, a pyramidal structure of conferences and committees replaces the usual chain of command. In others, impersonal measures of productivity are substituted for direct supervision. Several influential movements like group dynamics and sensitivity training have a psychoanalytic flavor; they identify the desire to exercise direct authority as a neurosis and undertake to cure it by group therapy. "Having a position of domi-nance," wrote Elliott Jaques in *The Changing Culture of a Factory*, "stirs latent wishes to dominate for the sake of power itself as well as for the requirements of the job. But, to the extent that dominance is used for personal gratification, a profound sense of guilt ensues."[11]

The principle that authority can be enhanced by giving it away is central to modern management, but it does have certain limitations that prevent it from being universally applied. In many operations, the need for precise coordination among the parts of an organization is so compelling that it takes precedence over the improvement of morale or productivity. Most large organizations include some oper-ating units that are not fully committed to the organizational program and that are more likely to use an increase of autonomy to sabotage their tasks than to perform them with heightened zeal.

Another limitation of the human relations approach is that subor-dinates as well as managers are capable of learning that the delega-tion of authority may be used to enhance a manager's power, what Peter Drucker calls "psychological despotism."[12] The manipulations of a manager oriented to human relations may be resisted as stub-bornly as the arm-twisting of an old-fashioned authoritarian. Some workers would rather be ruled by a drillmaster than by a psychiatric social worker.

There are situations in which neither of these types of leadership is appropriate. Gordon Tullock in *The Politics of Bureaucracy* ana-lyzes the situation of an infantry commander in combat, when he wants something other than simple obedience from his subordinate officers.

> What the captain wants from the patrol commanders is not the simple and uncomplicated obedience which we find on the drill ground, but something much more difficult to obtain. The captain wants the leaders of his patrols to reach decisions on the host of problems with which they will be confronted which will conform to his general strategy; but he can-not tell in advance what their decisions will be like. In this situation the company commander is making an attempt to multiply his mental powers by giving a task to subordinates which requires that they think and act on their own. . . .
>
> The patrol situation has the advantage over the parade ground situation in that far more decisions can be made by the whole organization because each of the subordinates must reach decisions in addition to the single su-perior. The disadvantage is that some of the decisions made by the sub-ordinates will inevitably be contrary to the desires of the commander.[13]

There may be other disadvantages to the delegation of authority, as when subordinate managers acquire so much autonomous authority that the central organization is unable to suppress conflicts between them. When subordinate managers are weak, they will not work effectively for the organization, but when they are too strong, they cannot easily be restrained from fighting each other. A state of baronial warfare does not prevent mutinous coalitions against the ruler. Indeed, it makes such coalitions more likely.

The principle that a manager should delegate as much authority as possible to subordinate managers obviously needs to be hedged with reservations. The manager should do so only if (a) his or her control of the organization's finances is secure; (b) the performance of operating departments can be objectively measured; (c) there are no obvious conflicts of interest between operating departments and the central organization; (d) the subordinate manager is not now and has never been an active candidate for the top position; and (f) the subordinate manager is not irremovable because of formal tenure or informal influence.

A headquarters staff, as we noted before, cannot function well except as a council, and it is a constant concern of the manager to encourage informal communication among the staff advisers. Nearly the opposite rule applies to subordinate managers, who are asked to be competitive without flying at each other's throats. Excessive communication among them multiplies the opportunities for destructive conflict and the parallel opportunities for improper coalitions. Most exceptions are only apparent. In the United States government, for example, the President's cabinet, composed of the heads of major departments, is an advisory council in theory, but every effective President has turned elsewhere for assistance in decision-making.

Dealing with the Rank-and-File

In most instances, this level of the organization is much more heavily populated than the others—the workers of a factory, the soldiers of an army, the clerks of a bureaucracy.

In many organizations there are two distinct levels of the rank-and-file: the lowest category of organizational functionaries and, below them, a category of clients—for example, welfare recipients—who must be considered because, unlike the guests of a hotel or the patrons of a theater, they are locked into the organization and subject to its authority.

Tables of organization often omit clients altogether because they are not paid, but provided that the clients are routinely dependent on the organization and subject to managerial authority, they ought to be included. Thus, a school has a rank-and-file of classroom teachers and another rank-and-file of pupils; a welfare agency has a rank-and-file of social workers and another of beneficiaries; a hospital has its rank-and-file of aides and attendants and another rank-and-file of patients.

Many rank-and-files have spokesmen who represent their interests vis-à-vis management—shop stewards, walking delegates, prefects, tribunes of the people, and outside representatives of various kinds. Rank-and-file spokesmen are nearly always omitted from the table of organization, but this does not in any way diminish their importance in real life, and the manager who does not find them on the chart must still find out who they are, what they do, what occasions bring them out, and what they expect from him or her.

In a small organization, such as a symphony orchestra or an elementary school, the manager may spend a large part of the working day in direct contact with the rank-and-file. In a larger organization, such as a factory or a military base, the manager's contact with the rank-and-file is likely to be very limited, and he is likely to have a sense of isolation from them and to rely excessively on his few contacts with low-ranking members of the organization, like chauffeurs and elevator operators, or with other rank-and-file people he knows personally.

The reason there is so little contact between the manager and the rank-and-file in some organizations is that such contact is not required by the organizational program. As manager, you are supposed to communicate with staff officials and subordinate managers who, in turn, communicate with the rank-and-file. William Whyte's classic study of a street-corner gang in an Italian slum in Boston (described in his *Street Corner Society*) showed that although the gang had only about a dozen members, the leader's relationship with the rank-and-file was conducted almost exclusively through intermediaries.[14] Even in an organization of this miniature scale, it was possible to identify the staff officials and subordinate managers through whom the leader's communications with the seven or eight young men who composed the rank-and-file were transmitted.

Although the manager and the rank-and-file may see very little of each other, the relationship is important to both parties. In a crisis, the manager's ability to understand and to be understood by the rank-and-file often makes the difference between success and failure.

For the rank-and-file, the responsible manager is a living symbol of the organization's collective identity. Any honor or disgrace he incurs affects them all. Even the manager of a supermarket has some dim trace of the aura that surrounds monarchs, ship captains, senior partners of law firms, and museum curators. You may continue to enjoy the loyalty of the rank-and-file if you are corrupt or cruel or technically incompetent, but you will lose them at once if you show any sign of not taking the organization seriously, not caring about its reputation or not attaching any importance to your own prerogatives.

Besides this symbolic function as King of the Lions, the manager of an organization has practical duties in relation to the rank-and-file. You are, or should be, their principal source of information about the organization's purposes and policies and whatever changes occur in them. You are, or should' be, their ultimate guarantor of justice; that is, of the equitable application of rules to individuals. In most well-run organizations, this means that some procedure is provided whereby an action that adversely affects any member of the organization can be appealed directly or indirectly to the top and can be nullified either for good cause, which is one sort of justice, or out of compassion, which is another sort of justice. Even if these managerial prerogatives are seldom exercised, it is essential that they exist lest the organization appear as a heartless monster, incapable of remorse or sympathy. In nearly all organizations the manager distributes promotions and rewards in his own name, if not on his own initiative.

The ritualistic nature of the relationship between the manager and the rank-and-file impedes the flow of information upward. Every manager needs to know about some events at the rank-and-file level; for example, you would like to learn about any dramatic change in your own popularity, or the popularity of a subordinate manager, before rebellion erupts.

This information will not come to you spontaneously in even the smallest organization. Active steps must be taken to obtain it. The method of Caliph Haroun Al-Raschid, whereby the ruler disguises himself and wanders among his subjects, is one of the best, but it can only be practiced by very self-confident rulers in very large organizations.

The difficulty experienced by many managers in obtaining a steady flow of information from the rank-and-file is related to one of the most fundamental problems of management: the tension inherent in the relationship between superiors and subordinates. To this irremovable problem and some of its partial solutions we now turn.

How to Interact Comfortably with Subordinates

As a manager, all of your human contacts inside the organization are with subordinates, since you have no peers and no superiors there. Unless you can get along comfortably with subordinates you will never be able to do your job well or enjoy it. Otherwise, like Julius Caesar and the last shah of Iran, your situation may be hopeless by the time you find out that you are in trouble. Some people take to this situation more readily than others, but even very timid and self-conscious people can do very well in unequal relationships if they understand how the interaction between a subordinate and a superior differs from other human relationships and why a given conversation between a superior and a subordinate seldom evokes the same sentiments from both.

If we go into any organization and quietly observe the relationship between a superior and a subordinate for several weeks or months, we discover that most of their conversations are initiated by the subordinate, while most of the activity resulting from those conversations is initiated by the superior. Typically, the subordinate, having finished an assignment or run into a problem, goes to the superior and says, "This is the position. What shall I do now?"—thus initiating a conversation. At the end of the conversation the superior says something like, "Why don't you try using the thingamabob?"—thus initiating an activity. The frequency *and* the content of these conversations are usually set by the subordinate, who makes a complicated calculation in doing so. The fewer of these conversations he has, the more autonomous he will be in carrying out his organizational tasks but the less help he will receive with them. Faced with this Hobson's choice, most subordinates in most organizations choose autonomy and minimize contact with their superiors. An important minority of subordinates choose to maximize their contacts with their superiors either because they think themselves too weak to function autonomously or strong enough to gain more than they lose by putting themselves under close supervision.

This choice can be observed in a very wide range of situations, from the grade school class in which a majority of pupils avoid close contact with the teacher while a minority of teacher's pets seek her out, to the multinational corporation in which most managers try to keep as much social and geographical distance as possible between themselves and the home office while a few appear there at every opportunity. A competent teacher will try hard to draw the isolated pupil closer and even harder to discourage the excessive dependence of the teacher's pet. A competent corporate manager will act similarly.

This is often more easily said than done, if only because of the sociopsychological illusion whereby we perceive extraneous conversation in a working relationship as a sign of friendliness. This perception is roughly accurate in relationships among peers or in casual relationships where there is nothing to be gained from extraneous conversation besides the pleasure of sociability. In conversations between superiors and subordinates, although sociability plays a part, the participants always have ulterior motives, which makes it impossible for either party to interpret the sentiments of the other by so easy an index.

It is much better practice for you to measure the affection of your subordinates by their zeal to comply with your orders than by their eagerness to fraternize with you.

Even with this austere criterion, a new manager is likely to misidentify friends and enemies among his subordinates until he has had a long and varied experience with them. The superior and subordinate who interact frequently learn a great deal about each other, but each of them gets a different type of information. The superior gets a comprehensive view of the subordinate's performance because he sees it from above, can compare it with the performance of the subordinate's peers, and has a license to examine any aspect of the performance on behalf of the organization. The subordinate has a much hazier view of the superior's performance, much of which does not concern him or her at all, or is responsive to demands that he or she knows nothing about, or is judged by standards with which he or she has no reason to be familiar. The kindergarten teacher can evaluate the pupils' performance quite easily, while the pupils have no way of judging the effectiveness of the teacher aside from whether they like or dislike him or her.

To compensate for the subordinate's tunnel vision with respect to the competence of the superior, he or she gets to know a great deal about the superior as a person without being required to reveal very much in return. The superior ordinarily has no means of obtaining information about the habits or attitudes of a subordinate except by unaided observation, and what that observation can yield is severely limited by the subordinate's inclination to dissemble emotions and conceal events to which the superior might react unfavorably. The superior has less motive for personal concealment, since the subordinate's judgments are less threatening to him than his own judgments to the subordinate; but even if he wanted to conceal himself, he has no way of shutting off the subordinate's exchange of information with other people in the organization to whom the superior is an object of constant interest and observation.

All that you as a manager can do about this is to follow certain prudent rules that take into account this disparity of perspective between you and your subordinates. One such rule is to mistrust your own opinions and judgments about subordinates in matters that are unrelated to their work or go beyond it. As manager, you cannot ever tell with certainty, for example, whether your assistants are happy to see you or not. Nor can you ever hope to understand the office love affairs that are crystal clear to everyone else. Don't try very hard to share in the network of gossip and news; at best you will remain ignorant of matters that everyone else knows about, and at worst your participation in the grapevine may be used to manipulate your judgment of people and events. You also need to remember that, while you cannot see through the veils worn by your subordinates, your own face is always under scrutiny from multiple points of observation, so that any attempt to present different faces to different people may expose you to ridicule.

There is another imbalance built into the emotional exchange between a superior and a subordinate. Under most circumstances their interaction makes much more difference for the subordinate than for the superior, if only because the subordinate has more to hope for by way of reward and more to fear by way of punishment. The sentiments of superiors to subordinates normally vary from friendly to hostile, while the sentiments of subordinates to superiors are often ambivalent, including both friendly and unfriendly feelings at the same time.

Of course, this pattern may be reversed or modified in particular cases. There are traces of ambivalence in every cooperative relationship, and acute ambivalence may be felt on either side of a relationship. But the susceptibility of subordinates to ambivalent feelings about superiors needs to be reckoned with in every organization. The reasons are self-evident. The subordinate is, among other things, an instrument for the achievement of the superior's purposes and is

	Superior Observing Subordinate	Subordinate Observing Superior
Evaluating performance	Has much information	Has little information
Explaining motives	Has little information	Has much information

liked or loved if he fulfills that function and disliked or hated if he fails to do so. The superior, by contrast, is a source of both rewards and frustrations for the subordinate, and he influences the subordinate's happiness more than his own is affected in return.

The usual reaction of an ambivalent subordinate is to display affection and conceal resentment in the presence of the superior. When you must work with a number of subordinates in the same situation, they will probably compete in expressing loyalty to your face, and exchange grievances behind your back.

There is no need for you to be alarmed by this prospect. It is a wholesome condition and will do you no harm provided you do not allow yourself to be lulled into the illusion that you are universally loved. That illusion—the occupational disease of tyrants—is certain to get you into trouble sooner or later when you discover perfidious sentiments among your followers or count too heavily upon their loyalty in a crisis. *"Et tu, Brute"* is the perennial complaint of managers who do not take the ambivalence of their subordinates into account. The wiser ruler enjoys and reciprocates the expressions of devotion he receives, but omits them from his tactical calculations.

Taking Account of Third Parties

The relationship between a superior and a subordinate is further complicated by the curious catalytic effects that occur in such relationships in the presence of third parties, especially when the third parties belong to the same hierarchy. The general pattern of these effects is summed up in the table below, although there are innumerable variations and nuances.

How the Presence of a Third Party Affects the
Interaction between a Superior and a Subordinate

Third Party Present	Communication between Superior and Subordinate	Authority of Superior Over Subordinate	Emotional Solidarity of Superior and Subordinate
Superior's superior	Much less	Much more	More
Superior's peer	Less	More	Less
Intervening subordinate	Less	More	Much Less
Subordinate's peer	Less	Less	Much less
Subordinate's subordinate	Much less	Less	More
Outsider	Less	More	More

The first column of the table shows what happens to the interaction between a superior and a subordinate in the presence of a third party. (The table refers in each case to a single third party; multiple third parties usually influence the relationship in the same direction but more forcefully.) As communication decreases, interaction becomes more formal and less spontaneous, tongues are guarded, emotions are censored, and interaction approaches the minimum required by the organization program. The influence of third parties on communication between superior and subordinate is dismayingly simple—the presence of *any* third party decreases it, although the intensity of the effect varies according to the identity of the third party.

This effect has all sorts of practical implications for any manager. Whenever you want to hold a candid conversation with a subordinate, you had better arrange to hold it privately. When you need to have such conversations with a number of subordinates, you had better see them one by one, even if it takes more time and trouble than you like. The inhibiting effect of a third party is an automatic feature of the situation; it is not under the control of the people involved, and it cannot be suppressed by an effort of will. Busy managers often try to override the mechanism by ignoring the presence of a third party who is unavoidably present at a discussion but has no special interest in the matter discussed. It cannot be done. A conversation that pretends to be private is always less informative than one that *is* private.

The second column of the table shows a somewhat more intricate set of effects. The pressure on a subordinate to conform to the authority of a superior is usually enhanced by the presence of another superior, even of a person to whom the subordinate never reports. The bosses, the subordinate might say, gang up on him. This, too, is an automatic mechanism. When, as sometimes happens, it fails to work, the failure signals a breakdown in the hierarchical structure.

The presence of outsiders—those not in the hierarchy—has a similar effect. The superior's authority is usually reinforced, either because the outsider represents a larger social system to which the whole organization belongs, or in order to maintain normal appearances, as Erving Goffman shows in his *Relations in Public*.[15]

The presence of the subordinate's peers or subordinates has an opposite effect on the superior's authority, strengthening the subordinate's ability to resist, and restricting the scope of obedience the superior can demand.

Although this model is almost excessively simple, it seems to work most of the time. An interesting study of a military unit by Reece McGee found that the mere number of superiors, peers, and subordinates with whom an officer routinely interacted went a long way toward explaining how the officer was rated on efficiency and leadership.[16] In general, the more superiors an officer had to deal with, the harder he found it to appear efficient; the more peers he had to back him up, and the more subordinates he had to help him with his assignments, the easier it was to make a good showing.

Most managers apply the principles stated above by intuition, individualizing their interaction with subordinates when they anticipate resistance and associating themselves with superiors and outsiders when they are not sure of obtaining compliance otherwise. But, if the purpose of such a maneuver becomes apparent, it is likely to fail. Juggling the audience to minimize the possibility that subordinates will defy his authority is something every manager has to do from time to time; the skill consists in doing it unobtrusively, so that the appearance or disappearance of third parties around the scene of action is attributable to other causes.

The last column of the table shows the normal effect of the presence of third parties on the emotional solidarity of a superior and a subordinate. This follows a different pattern. The parties to an unequal relationship, like human actors everywhere, are drawn closer together by the presence of people who are different from themselves and potentially unfriendly, and are pulled apart by the appearance of rivals for each other's affections. In an organizational setting, the sense of solidarity between a superior and a subordinate is strengthened by the presence of persons who are superior to both of them, subordinate to both of them, or altogether outside of their hierarchy. In the presence of a general, sergeants and privates stand together. Surrounded by civilians, the general and the enlisted men may feel a surprising warmth toward each other as fellow soldiers.

Coping with Coalitions

That extraordinarily original scholar Georg Simmel was the first sociologist to observe the systematic tendency of social groups made up of three actors—either individual or collective actors—to split into a combination of two against one. The combination of two is called a coalition, and the group of three in which it occurs is called a triad. The study of coalitions within triads fascinates modern sociologists because of the precision and regularity of the coalition-forming process and the ease with which complex social systems can be reduced to triadic form for analytical purposes.[17] The point of such analyses is to explain how power is transformed into weakness, and weakness into power, by the shifting coalitions within a social system.

Triads can be classified according to the relative power of their members into eight patterns, which seem to be found in all human societies. In relation to problems of management, the most important of these types is the hierarchical triad diagrammed in Figure 3.

In this triad, A is stronger than either B or C and dominates either of them alone, but B and C together are stronger than A. When A is a manager and BC are the two leading subordinates, A's problem is how to avoid the formation of the rebellious coalition BC. Almost any managerial situation can evolve into a pattern in which the manager confronts two subordinates capable of resisting his authority if they decide to combine against him. Captain Bligh's authority overawes

Figure 3. Coalitions in a Hierarchial Triad

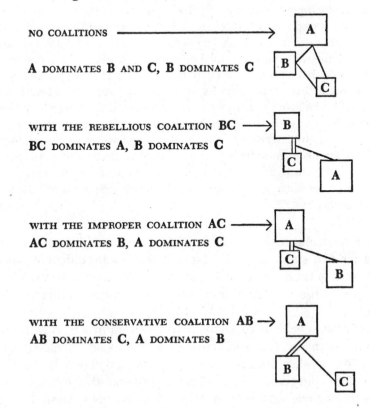

NO COALITIONS

A DOMINATES B AND C, B DOMINATES C

WITH THE REBELLIOUS COALITION BC
BC DOMINATES A, B DOMINATES C

WITH THE IMPROPER COALITION AC
AC DOMINATES B, A DOMINATES C

WITH THE CONSERVATIVE COALITION AB
AB DOMINATES C, A DOMINATES B

Mr. Christian and the bosun separately, but if they combine against him, they are strong enough to put him over the side.

Even a manager who has overwhelming authority and cannot be overthrown must still reckon with the respectful coalitions formed by subordinates, but the problems with those are relatively trivial compared to the problem of protecting himself against a rebellious coalition. In most organizations, the art of management consists to a large extent of preventing rebellious coalitions.

Long ago Simmel saw how dangerous a triad, composed of a superior and two equal subordinates, can be for the superior and how it converts his strength to weakness by inviting the formation of a coalition which renders him helpless. Simmel's solution was to make B and C slightly unequal.

It was the general custom of the Incas to divide a newly conquered tribe in two approximately equal halves and to place a supervisor over each of them, but to give these two supervisors slightly different ranks. This was indeed the most suitable means for provoking rivalry between the two heads, which prevented any united actions against the ruler on the part of the subjected territory. By contrast, both identical ranks and greatly different ranks would have made identification much easier. If the two heads had had the same rank, an equal distribution of leadership in case of action would have been more likely than other arrangement; and, since there would have been need for subordination, peers would have most probably submitted to such a technical necessity. If the two heads had had very different ranks, the leadership of one would have found no opposition. The slight difference in rank least of all allows an organic and satisfactory arrangement in the unification feared, since the one would doubtless have claimed unconditional prerogative because of his superiority, which, on the other hand, was not significant enough to suggest the same claim to the other.[18]

Modern managers share the same perception, and it is rather unusual for two strong subordinates to remain substantially equal for any length of time. Even a weak, ineffectual manager can usually arrange to tip the balance of authority toward one subordinate or the other.

Of course, rebellious coalitions may also form in a triad with three unequal members, but a BC coalition is not as advantageous for C when C is weaker than B. C gains ascendancy over A by joining a BC coalition but remains subordinate to B within the coalition, sometimes trading one master for another. This may not be desirable from his standpoint. C shares the unavoidable risks of rebellion equally with B but does not profit equally.

One alternative for C when offered a BC coalition is to form an AC coalition instead, for while subordinate to his partner in that coalition also, C will gain an ascendancy over B that he did not have before, without running any of the risks attached to rebellion against A.

The process whereby triads split into a division of two-against-one has been extensively studied in laboratory experiments. In the typical experiment, three subjects are asked to play a game or solve a problem that has been carefully arranged to make them unequal in power, and their behavior is observed through a one-way mirror and recorded by various instruments. A series of such experiments by many investigators has confirmed the existence of a tendency for the two weaker members of a hierarchical triad to combine against the stronger member by forming a BC coalition. The probability of a BC coalition is not constant, however. It varies from one experimental game to another, and it can be manipulated by modifying the rules and conditions.

The reliable expectation in a hierarchical triad is that *some* coalition will be formed. The threat of a BC coalition is too much for A to live with indefinitely—particularly when considering that B stands to gain so much from a rebellious coalition that B may be willing to offer equality to C in order to gain C's adherence. At the same time, B is acutely aware that an AC coalition will make him low man in the triad without much cost to either A or C, and if he cannot have a BC coalition, B probably prefers an AB coalition to none at all.

What should A do in this situation, assuming that he cannot reduce the strength of B or C enough to make a BC coalition ineffectual? If he can do that, he may want to. But if he cannot, he is well advised to form a coalition with either B or C before they sign up with each other.

Which one does A choose? The AC coalition is tempting. C is more eager to join A than is B, who has his heart set on the BC coalition. C, being weaker than B, will probably be a more tractable partner. Since B poses more of a threat to A's authority, it may seem imprudent to strengthen him further by an AB coalition. Nevertheless, in nine cases out of ten, the right choice for the manager in a hierarchical triad is to form the AB coalition if possible. It is the only coalition that does not undermine the table of organization or interfere with the organization's program, and the manager ought to prefer it as a matter of principle. The manager is more likely to gain than to lose by upholding the authority of his principal subordinate.

The AC coalition, sometimes called an improper coalition, preserves A's authority at the cost of creating an ambiguous relationship between B and C. B continues to claim authority over C as an individual but is dominated by the AC coalition, in which C is a partner. Under this arrangement, neither B nor C can exercise authority with any confidence, and the organizational program for which the triad is responsible is sure to suffer.

Crisis Management

If you, the new manager, do not establish your authority early, the chance of your doing it later is exceedingly thin. Conversely, once your authority is established, it probably tends to persist as long as you continue in good health and take your work seriously *if* you are able to cope with crises as they arise. Regardless of how long and well they have handled their routine responsibilities, nearly all managers must sometimes confront a major crisis that puts their authority in question.

Some people's routines, as Everett Hughes has remarked, consist of dealing with other people's emergencies. An organization that handles emergencies routinely does not define them as crises. A fire is not ordinarily a crisis for a fire department but any fire is a crisis for a school, and if an alarm is sent out for a school fire and the firemen cannot respond because of an equipment breakdown, that is a crisis for the fire department.

An organizational crisis is a problem that calls for maximum effort. The manager's role in eliciting this maximum effort is both symbolic and practical. Symbolically, he personifies the organization's determination to solve the problem and provides a model of energy and devotion for other members to imitate. Practically, he is responsible for the temporary social structure that every real crisis requires and for overseeing it until the crisis has passed.

Time being always of the essence in crisis, it is convenient to describe the manager's response as a sequence of seven stages:

1. recognize that a crisis exists

2. appear on the scene

3. recruit a crisis council

4. mobilize resources

5. enact a plan

6. announce the outcome

7. distribute rewards

Your recognition of a crisis in the organization should be dramatic, instantaneous, and unmistakable. When the news arrives in the middle of the night, it is seldom advisable to wait until morning to react. There is very little danger in wrongly identifying a noncrisis as a crisis; it will give everyone concerned an interlude of pleasurable excitement and probably be remembered as a crisis surmounted. There is always grave danger in responding too slowly or too feebly to a crisis announcement. By morning the situation may be irretrievable.

As soon as a crisis has been recognized, you must get to its scene, even if the crisis is inconveniently located or you have better facilities for working on it somewhere else. Any long delay in appearing on the scene is likely to destroy your authority, regardless of the eventual outcome of the crisis. I have known the manager of an international enterprise to lose control of it because when one of his subordinates was missing at sea in a disabled company boat, he directed rescue operations from the home office instead of going to the port from which the search was being conducted. The search was successful, but the stay-at-home manager never recovered his authority in that part of the world. The local impression was that he had been neg-lectful. In other instances, the manager's absence from the scene convicts him of timidity or cowardice. The college president who will not come out of his office to face a student riot but sends a dean in his place might as well resign then and there instead of waiting to discover that his usefulness is ended.

Once on the scene, you may find yourself in the peculiar position of having to sustain a mood of urgency without doing very much. The obvious steps—putting in the fire alarm, closing the driveway to traffic, getting the cash out of the safe, finding the night watchman—are likely to have been taken already. The less obvious steps that will need to be taken require more information and advice than are yet available. It is at this point that you should recruit a crisis council to stay in session until the crisis is over. You are free to name anyone in the organization to that council, but in most instances there are certain people who must be included if the council is to have quick and frictionless access to the needed facilities. In a small organiza-tion, the crisis council may have only two or three members, but the council assembled by President Kennedy for the Cuban missile crisis included about fifty officials of varying rank and function who spent nearly twenty-four hours a day for more than two weeks working to-gether in the White House in close contact with the President until the crisis was over.[19] A crisis council is almost always more demo-cratic than the table of organization from which its members are drawn. In the ideal case, the members treat each other as equals in the development of information, advice, and alternative contingency plans for the manager's consideration. When the opinion of the coun-cil on any point is unanimous, it prevails; when there is a division of opinion in the council, the manager can follow the advice of either the majority or the minority without expecting resistance.

One of the first recommendations of a crisis council is likely to be a mobilization. All sorts of people and facilities are made ready to be used in contingencies that will probably not occur. This move, too, has both symbolic and practical purposes. Symbolically, it announces the fateful character of the organization's struggle for survival and the temporary suspension of other organizational goals. Practically, it enlarges the manager's ability to respond to unforeseen events and to deploy resources in new combinations.

The next stage in the management of the crisis is the enactment of a plan. What that plan will be about depends, of course, on the nature of the crisis; it may be a battle or an election, a championship game or a corporate takeover, a budget hearing or a hurricane, a strike or a schism. The common principles that apply to these diverse events are few but important. First, any plan is better than moment-to-moment improvisation. Second, once a plan has been adopted, all the weight of the organization should be thrown behind it. Third, every crisis plan should include provision for the worst possible outcome, starting from Murphy's law ("Whatever can go wrong, will") and including some provisions for each of Murphy's contingencies.

Terminating a crisis promptly, once the danger has passed, is nearly as important as recognizing it promptly. This is the step most often scanted. Flushed by success and exhausted by their efforts, the members of the crisis council return to their normal duties, leaving their organizational audience in confusion. (The reserve units called up during the Cuban missile crisis were not sent home until many months later.) The right procedure is to wind the crisis up, dissolving the crisis council, demobilizing the reserves, evaluating the outcome, and distributing rewards or thanks to those who served and those who only stood and waited.

None of the foregoing advice is meant to contradict the suggestion made in the Introduction that a good manager ought to have few organizational crises and ought to prepare for them long in advance. Nevertheless, in most organizations it is nearly impossible for a manager to make his authority secure until he has surmounted at least one major crisis.

How to Recognize Secure Authority

The marks of secure authority differ somewhat from one type of organization to another and according to managerial styles, but there are certain neat little clues which always identify the manager whose authority is secure. You must be able to say yes to most of the following questions:

1. Do your subordinates come to you for advice and instruction on routine matters without being sent for?

2. Can you make suggestions to subordinates that are not misconstrued as orders?

3. Can you go anywhere in the organization without fear or embarrassment?

4. Do you get along well with the people who are just below you in the table of organization?

5. Do you miss most of the gossip about the private lives of people in the organization?

6. Are the matters referred to you for decision those you want referred while subordinates make other decisions on their own?

7. When you return to the organization after an absence, do you expect to find things quiet and peaceful?

8. Do rank-and-file members of the organization seem genuinely pleased when they run into you unexpectedly?

9. When you preside at a meeting of subordinates, can you get them to talk freely?

10. Are you able, at such a meeting, to suspend the discussion of a controversial topic and go on to something else?

11. When you attend a meeting presided over by one of your subordinates, does it run quite normally?

12. Can you make promotions, appointments, or expenditures without consulting anybody except those people with whom the table of organization requires you to consult?

13. Can you adjust your personal workload upward or downward without adversely affecting the organization?

14. Is there less turnover and absenteeism among your close associates than elsewhere in the organization?

15. Are you able to prevent rebellious coalitions and to stay out of improper coalitions?

CHAPTER TWO

Communication

The Guv'nor addresses:

Co-Director Michael Yates as Mike
Assistant Director Michael Yates as Michael
Sectional Manager Michael Yates as Mr. Yates
Sectional Assistant Michael Yates as Yates
Apprentice Michael Yates as Michael
Night-watchman Michael Yates as Mike

Stephen Potter

Building a Consensus

The manager's task of holding the organization together requires an adequate flow of information upward and downward, and inward and outward. The adequacy of this information flow is measured by the consensus that results from it; that is, the extent to which members of the organization come to agree about the organization's goals.

With high consensus, an organization will have few quarrels; with intermediate consensus, there will be many quarrels, but most of them will be resolved or contained; with low consensus, there will be frequent and severe conflicts and any one of them may turn into a disaster.

Communication and consensus are intimately related, but the relationship is too complex to be reduced to a simple formula. On the one hand, the improvement of consensus ordinarily requires increased communication. On the other hand, an increase in the flow of information between two parts of an organization can undermine an existing consensus.

Every organization can be analyzed as a communication network, as Chester Barnard showed long ago in a book called *The Functions of the Executive.*[1] Networks of this kind are fascinating. They come in all sorts of shapes—pyramidal, serial, circular, radial—and in all sizes, and they use a variety of devices to code and transmit information. The analysis of the multiple factors that affect the efficiency of a communication network—such as physical distance, social distance, commonality of language, extraneous noise, authentication, and circuit design—is always interesting.

The practical problems of communication that every active manager must face present themselves in simpler form. The questions you might ask yourself look like this:

1. How can the routine reports I receive about the organization's activities be made more reliable, accurate, and comprehensive?

2. With whom should I consult before making decisions? Who should I inform about decisions after they are made?

3. What information do I need to keep secret? How?

4. How much attention should I give to rumormongers and talebearers? What use, if any, should I make of spies?

5. How should I go about repairing or replacing parts of the communications network that have broken down?

6. How can I make my nonverbal gestures mean what I want them to mean to the organizational audience?

In actual experience, these six questions and their answers are inextricably entwined, but for purposes of discussion it is convenient to consider them separately.

Routine Reports

The easiest way to make your mark as a manager is to improve the quality of the routine reports the organization produces—hourly, daily, weekly, monthly, quarterly, annually; in written, graphic, or numerical form—about its ongoing activities. This is often quite easy to do, because there are very few people who grasp the importance of routine reporting and even fewer who understand how to set up appropriate reporting procedures. Systems of routine reporting deteriorate in use, so that even the best system needs to be reformed from time to time.

The first step in setting up or reforming a system of routine reports is to determine priorities. Top-priority reports are those that claim attention as soon as they appear. Middle-priority reports are needed for occasional reference. Low-priority reports refer to matters that do not ordinarily require action.

A good deal of care, and as much expense as necessary, ought to be lavished on the production of top-priority reports. It goes without saying that reports in this category should be as prompt, accurate, and complete as is humanly possible, and that they should be in a form that permits comparison with other organizations, with past performance, and with projected achievements.

As usual, it may be helpful to visualize a concrete case. Let us use a public high school for this purpose and assume that you are the principal.

The most important routine report that comes to your desk is the daily attendance report (see Figure 4), which shows the number of students and teachers present and absent by class and grade, together with absentees and the number of persons who have joined or left the roster since the previous day. A well-designed reporting form (Figure 4) ought to provide a summary absenteeism rate for the entire school and the corresponding rates for yesterday, last week, and a year ago.

If records of lateness are kept, you might be tempted to add a comparable summary of lateness to the daily attendance report, but unless lateness has some special local significance, the temptation should be resisted. Lateness and absenteeism are both good (negative) indicators of morale, but they are so closely related that only the absenteeism rate need be calculated. For both the producers and the users of a routine report, it is nearly as important to keep superfluous information out as to get essential information in. By the way, when computers are used, this is much harder to do.

Let us assume that school begins every morning at 8:30. The daily attendance report, preferably on a single sheet of paper, ought to come to you by 9:30. Like most top-priority reports, it has multiple functions. If the report is usually on time and complete, you are likely to take its accuracy for granted after a while. But you ought not to do so since, in the first place, reports of human behavior are inherently fallible and, in the second place, systems of routine reporting tend to deteriorate. You must remind yourself to verify the information in the daily attendance report from time to time and to raise a terrible fuss whenever you find an error. The enumeration of absentees can be

Figure 4

CENTRAL HIGH SCHOOL

Daily Attendance Report

For: _____   Prepared by: _____
   Day   Date

		TEACHER	ABS	ROSTER	LATE	ABSENT TODAY	ABSENT YESTER-DAY
Grade 9	Class	9a Benedict	( )	____	____	____	____
		9b Winther	( )	____	____	____	____
		9c Williamson	( )	____	____	____	____
		9d Field	( )	____	____	____	____
Grade 10	Class	10a Kranich	( )	____	____	____	____
		10b Doubleday	( )	____	____	____	____
		10c Kantor	( )	____	____	____	____
Grade 11	Class	11a Binno	( )	____	____	____	____
		11b Potvin	( )	____	____	____	____
		11c Hubers	( )	____	____	____	____
Grade 12	Class	12a Arb	( )	____	____	____	____
		12b Lambij	( )	____	____	____	____
		12c Otter	( )	____	____	____	____
Ungraded Class		Christian	( )	____	____	____	____
		SCHOOL TOTALS	____	____	____	____	____

CUMULATIVE ABSENCES TO THIS DATE _____

DITTO THIS DAY LAST YEAR _____

% ABSENT   TODAY _____

YESTERDAY _____

THIS DAY LAST WEEK _____

THIS DAY LAST YEAR _____

ADDITIONS TO ROSTER _____

SUBTRACTIONS FROM ROSTER _____

45

verified by going to a classroom and comparing the number of students physically present with the number listed as present. The total number present and absent in a given category can be compared with the number of names on the official roster. The arithmetic of totals and percentages can be verified by calculation. The figures for yesterday or last year may be checked against yesterday's or last year's reports in the files. Nit-picking procedures like these will not only help to keep the report trustworthy, they will also uncover anomalous and irregular situations of which you, the principal, should be aware.

Weekly reporting is relatively unimportant in a school; school weeks are of uneven length because of holidays, recesses, examinations, and other special events. Months are more significant. The principal's top-priority reports will certainly include a monthly attendance report; a monthly financial report that tells you where you are running ahead of or behind the budget; a utilities report summarizing the school's consumption of electricity, fuel, and telephone service and comparing current consumption with past and anticipated consumption; and an inventory report, showing supplies on hand. Unless this last report is carefully made and the movement of supplies in and out is just as carefully verified, pilferage is certain to flourish. You may well feel that your attention should be given to profound educational issues, but unless you are willing to endure the demoralization that accompanies waste and stealing, you had better give the utilities and inventory reports your full attention when they come to you.

The other significant reporting periods for a high school are the school term and the school year. Some reports are prepared both for the term and for the year; others for the year only. Just as the daily report generates a monthly report, so each monthly report generates a term report and an annual report. Some important reports are solely annual; for example, an academic achievement report, which shows the average grades assigned to students by level and subject, the average scores obtained by the students on standard achievement tests, the ratio of successful grade completions to the entering population of each grade, and the number of college applications and acceptances for the graduating class. This report, although complicated in appearance, is essential; without it, the school would fly blind.

We have lingered some time in the high school principal's office in order to show you how numerous and diverse are the minimum elements of information you need to do this job in a rational way. Most high schools do not have as good a system of routine reporting as the one outlined above. Instead, the principal receives a great volume of middle- and low-priority information that ought to stop lower down in the organization or not be gathered at all. Even a superficial analysis of the flow of paper in most high schools—and other organizations—will show people filling out forms in quintuplicate when one copy would be amply sufficient, keeping elaborate records for no purposes, obtaining redundant approval for routine actions, or preparing periodic reports that no one ever sees. It is only by pruning the overgrowth of red tape that the flowers of useful information can be made to grow.

In another type of organization, the routine reports that come to a manager might be more analytical and less descriptive. For example, an old study of the organizational performance of insurance agencies by Seashore and Yuchtman at the University of Michigan refers to such variables reported to agency managers as production costs per thousand dollars of insurance carried, maintenance costs per hundred dollars of premium collected, number of lives covered per one thousand insurables in the population, and so on for a total of seventy-six numerical indicators.[2] Curiously, however, the total volume of information required for effective management does not seem to vary in proportion to the size or complexity of the organization, if only because the ability of a single mind to absorb and remember information is limited. The larger the organization, the more severely must information be sifted and screened before it reaches the top. What happens then is pretty much the same in all well-run organizations: the report is scanned and its main outlines are remembered; occasionally some item stimulates further action.

The Art of Consultation

One of the most common managerial errors is the failure to consult someone who is entitled to be consulted about a particular matter. Just as it is said to be impossible to finish a sailboat race without making at least a few errors of judgment, so it is probably impossible to manage an organization without making some errors in consultation, but success usually goes to the skipper with the fewest errors.

The reason the art of consultation is so difficult is that it involves actions that run counter to the normal impulses of a good manager. Consultation interposes delays between the formulation and the execution of a project, elicits foolish and irrelevant objections, and leads to modifications that tarnish the original luster of the thing. Consultation with subordinates often *feels* uncomfortable. The manager has a sense of going hat in hand to beg or buy support he could as easily command. But nine times out of ten it will be better to suffer the discomfort of full consultation than to omit any part of it.

The most essential persons to be consulted in advance of a managerial decision are the subordinate managers and staff advisers and rank-and-file workers who will have to carry it out. The desirability of consulting those who are directly affected is self-evident: they are likely to have vital information about whether and how the decision can be implemented. Managers who don't get that information in advance are likely to make fools of themselves whenever they issue a directive, like the engineering executives in the machine shop studied by Donald Roy who periodically introduced new procedures that crippled production until the workmen evolved methods of circumventing them.[3]

But getting advice is only one of the twin purposes of consultation. The other and equally important purpose is to elicit consent. People are much more likely to support a decision they helped to make, or think they helped to make, than to support a decision imposed on them from above. This magic is so powerful that even an illusory participation in the making of a decision is often sufficient to secure the support of those who would otherwise oppose it.

It is possible to devise Machiavellian tricks that make use of this effect, for example, by putting obvious mistakes and defects into a proposal so that the people consulted will find it easy to make suggestions for improvement and to ascertain later that their suggestions have been followed. Even without such conniving, when the opponents of a project are seriously consulted and induced to participate in the planning stage, they often are irresistibly drawn toward the project despite their initial opposition.

Like most magic spells, this one can turn upon its user. The manager who seeks advice need not take it, but you must never seem to despise it. Hell hath no fury like a consultant scorned.

To consult all the subordinate managers and staff advisers directly affected by a prospective decision is hardly more than ordinary prudence. Consultation with those who may be indirectly affected is a more delicate operation. This sort of consultation runs the risk of arousing opposition in quarters where neither support nor opposition were called for. Nevertheless, because the indirect effects of decisions are so significant—as when the decision to expand one department of an organization is perceived as punitive by departments that are not expanded—the need for advice and consent often extends far beyond that part of an organization which seems to be directly concerned. A skillful manager will extend the consultation process as part as possible without creating needless problems, which is generally a good bit further than your natural inclination would take you.

There are several special types of consultation that call for some modification of the foregoing principles. Among these are consultation with committees, grievance procedures, consultation with outside experts, and consultation with the rank-and-file.

Consulting with Committees

The great comic theorist of organizations, Professor Parkinson, once suggested a formal study of committees to be known as "commitology," and mentioned in passing the fact that the world *committee* was originally singular and denoted a person appointed to represent the legal interests of a lunatic. The phenomenon is much older and wider than the word, however. Every organization, even a street-corner gang, seems to generate some committees. Large organizations have thousands of committees, with all sorts of administrative, judicial, and technical functions. We will confine our attention here to committees designed primarily for consultation. Within this category there are standing committees, special committees, and ad hoc committees.

The universal annoyance with committees is partly explained by the fact that so many committee meetings are occupied with business that is of little interest to the members. But from your standpoint as a manager, no meeting of a committee within your jurisdiction is really dull. The committee is an instrument that serves your interests much more than the interests of other members, no matter how democratic and egalitarian its proceedings may be.

Although commitology is not likely to become a recognized social science, there have been several excellent studies of how committees operate and what factors influence them—for example, the laboratory studies of Harold Guetzkow[4] and of James David Barber,[5] and the observational studies of Richard F. Fenno, Jr.,[6] and of Leonard Berkowitz.[7] The findings of these studies, taken together, suggest that committees with organizational tasks work best under a strong chairman who poses many questions, speaks more to the whole group than to individuals, defines the issues, keeps the discussion on its track, relates the amount of discussion to the available time, and attempts to arrive at group decisions. "There is a general expectation," writes Berkowitz in summarizing his study of seventy-two committees in business, industry, and government, "that the socially designated leader, the chairman, should be the sole major behavioral leader." He goes on to say that the sharing of leadership by other members seems to leave the members of a committee dissatisfied with each other and with their deliberations, regardless of whether the committee members who share leadership with the chairman are supporters or opponents. The empirical studies also seem to agree that successful chairmen do not attempt to prevent the expression of opposing viewpoints or to force a consensus prematurely. Several studies show that strong chairmen are better liked by their committees than passive chairmen, but also show that chairmen who are outranked by the members of their committees are likely to be passive.

These research results stand in apparent contradiction to what is sometimes called "sensitivity training," a method whereby people in large organizations are taught sensitivity in human relations as a means of developing "interpersonal competence." The formula for a successful sensitivity training group is nearly the opposite of the formula for a successful committee. The training group works best with a passive, permissive leader who makes no attempt to hold discussions to a fixed agenda or a definite time schedule, but encourages digressions that reveal the hidden emotions of the participants. This approach makes sense in its own context, which is closely related to group therapy, and the people who are sent by large organizations to participate in such training—for example, the government officials who attend the Federal Executive Institute in Charlottesville, Virginia—usually find the experience pleasant and educational. But those enthusiasts who attempt to impose the style of the training group on working committees in large organizations merely sow confusion.

How to Appoint Committees. A *standing committee* is a body with a continuous responsibility that calls for collective rather than individual judgment—for example, the rules committee of a legislature, the admissions committee of a college, the loan committee of a bank. As a rule of thumb, a standing committee should have a minimum of five members and a maximum of perhaps nine, although, of course, there are justifiable exceptions. The reason for the minimum of five is that it implies a working majority of three, which represents about as narrow a spread of collective judgment as can suffice in a situation that calls for collective judgment. The maximum of nine is a less rigid limit, but since most standing committees must meet regularly without the stimulus of an emergency, the difficulty of scheduling meetings for a larger number of people suggests an upper limit in this neighborhood unless the business of the committee is so overwhelmingly important that none of its members is likely to develop conflicting obligations.

As the manager of an organization, you ought never to appoint yourself as chairman of a standing committee. By doing so, you would defeat the purposes of such a committee, which are to relieve you of administrative burdens and to substitute a collective judgment for your individual judgment in certain recurrent, noncritical situations. It is usually a good idea, however, for you to be an ex officio member of any standing committee within your jurisdiction so as to have easy access to its deliberations and records when matters in which you are especially interested are considered.

The chairmen of standing committees ought to be senior to most of the other members, if only because they have to allocate work to them from time to time. They ought not to hold extreme opinions with respect to the area of interest, or be too new to the organization to understand its informal norms. The membership of a standing committee should be as broadly representative as its size permits, with regard to organizational rank, personal characteristics, and factional affiliations.

A *special committee* is typically appointed to consider some knotty problem that you, the manager, cannot resolve through your ordinary pattern of consultation because it is too complex, or too controversial, or too important to be handled in the regular way. Special committees are also appointed on occasion to delay an otherwise pressing decision, to deflect the onus of an unpopular decision, or to allay suspicions that have arisen in connection with a controversy. Some special committees are appointed to cope with problems that are intrinsically trivial but have acquired symbolic significance.

The membership of a special committee ought to be large enough to include all relevant shades of opinion and every important faction of the organization; the only upper limit is the capacity of the organization's largest conference table. A membership of twenty or twenty-five is not excessive. The best chairman for such a committee is a subordinate manager of considerable seniority, preferably with white hair and a good command of parliamentary procedure. The manager who appoints a special committee ought not to be a member of it, and

Rules of Thumb for Consulted Committees

Type of Committee	Size of Committee	Qualifications of Chairmen	Manager's Participation
Standing	5–9	Senior to most other members	As ex officio member
Special	10–30	Senior to all other members	Through informants
Ad hoc	2–5	Interested in assignment	None

unless you have some extraordinary announcement to make, you should never appear at its meetings or contribute to its deliberations once they have begun. You should, however, start the special committee off, describing its assignment in as much detail as necessary and indicating clearly what sort of report the committee is supposed to produce, within what interval of time, with what resources, and under what conditions of publicity or secrecy. It is permissible, and even conventional, for a manager to obtain access to the deliberations of a special committee by putting an assistant or a personal friend on it.

An *ad hoc committee* is ordinarily appointed for some noncontroversial, nonrecurrent task such as drafting a statement or inspecting an item offered for sale. A surprising proportion of ad hoc committees have three members; some have only two; five is about the practical maximum. It is important that the members of an ad hoc committee be compatible with each other and competent with respect to the committee's assignment. They do not need to be representative of the organization in any other way and it does not much matter which of them chairs the committee.

Conducting Committee Business. The manager who chairs a standing committee of his own organization is well advised to adopt a style that is simultaneously autocratic and permissive—autocratic with respect to controlling the agenda and determining the scope of the committee's responsibility for each agenda item, permissive in encouraging the free expression of opinions and in allowing room and time for a genuine consensus to develop, even if this means, as it frequently does, that decisions must be deferred from one meeting to the next and then possibly delayed again. A smooth-running committee of this kind may or may not vote formally on the matters before it, but nearly all of its decisions will be unanimous if only because the chairman insists on continuing the discussion of every matter until a sense of unanimity prevails.

Your relationship to committees you appoint but do not chair is somewhat different. Be well advised to adopt an attitude of deference toward such committees and to avoid the slightest appearance of interfering with their deliberations, since any action that they construe as interference is certain to be resented. For this reason, it is essential that when you appoint such a committee you retain a veto, either by stipulating in advance that the committee's decisions will be submitted to you as recommendations, or that they will not take effect until you have reviewed and approved them. This veto must be exercised from time to time even if you have no real objection to any of the committee's decisions, or the veto power will atrophy and may not be available when you need it.

The rule of noninterference with the deliberations of a committee does not prevent your attendance at meetings of a standing committee in the role of an ex officio member, provided you keep your mouth firmly shut except in response to direct questions. You should not attend the meetings of a special committee except in extraordinary circumstances.

In large organizations, the management of special committees is especially challenging. A special committee is usually appointed to resolve a complex and controversial problem. The resolution of such a problem usually has two stages: first, the development of a compromise that is acceptable to the members of the special committee; second, the acceptance of the compromise by the rest of the organization. A special committee that submits a majority report supported by only a bare majority must be regarded as a failure, and its report ought to be filed and forgotten. A committee that submits unanimous or nearly unanimous recommendations can be rated as successful, but it does not follow that its recommendations should be accepted forthwith. If, by accident or intent, the special committee did not include representatives of all the influential factions involved in the controversy, an acceptable compromise still remains to be achieved. If the special committee included speakers for opposed viewpoints, the production of a unanimous or nearly unanimous report ordinarily signifies that prolonged exposure to the facts of the situation and to each other has brought the factions within the special committee into agreement. The chances are, however, that in moving toward a common center, they have lost touch with the constituencies they were chosen to represent. The question of whether these constituencies will accept the compromise reached by their delegates has to be answered before the manager decides whether to implement, reject, or modify the committee's recommendation. For this question to be properly answered, the committee's report should be widely circulated within the organization and nothing else ought to be done about it for a while even though the problem is relatively urgent. When action is finally taken, it should be on the manager's responsibility and not the committee's. The best way to make this plain when acting on a special committee's recommendations is to modify them in some respects.

Grievance Procedures

The hearing of grievances is another type of managerial consultation. In many organizations, the grievance procedure is virtually the only channel through which the manager obtains information about morale, motivation, and conflict at lower levels of the organization. The settlement of grievances can be highly rewarding for both the manager and the organization, but it is intrinsically difficult and requires much more than simple goodwill.

A grievance is a complaint plus a request for redress. All organizations are full of complaints openly expressed to peers and sometimes to outsiders, but relatively few of them turn into grievances by being attached to a request for redress.

The nondirective interviews that were part of the famous Western Electric study collected eighty thousand complaints from workers in one industrial plant during a single year and classified them neatly into objectively verifiable complaints, subjective complaints, and nonlogical complaints. The Western Electric investigators concluded that: (1) the underlying attitude of the complainants toward their work and their associates was often more significant in accounting for complaints than the particular conditions complained of; (2) the mere opportunity to complain to a receptive listener connected with management had a favorable effect on morale; (3) after telling their complaints to the interviewer, workers often perceived an improvement in the condition complained about even though no objective change had occurred.[8] These effects have been confirmed in subsequent studies and used in organizational counseling programs. A particularly interesting factory study carried out in England by A. M. J. Sykes[9] showed that long-standing grievances held by workers against their foremen could be dissolved by a patterned system of eliciting and discussing complaints without changing the behavior of the foremen in any way.

The differences between such sociopsychological games and a genuine grievance procedure is that the latter, while still providing the benefits that seem to follow the airing of complaints, also requires management to do something about verifiable grievances and to attend to the real dissatisfactions that underline many imaginary grievances.

How many of an organization's circulating complaints turn into active grievances depends upon their volume and intensity, the receptivity of management to grievances, its reputation for fairness, the attitudes of particular managers, and the presence or absence of third parties. A high grievance rate is always a bad sign, but an abnormally low grievance rate is suspicious. Rensis Likert, in his *New Patterns of Management,* presented statistical evidence to show that industrial workers who are hostile to the enterprise in which they work seldom submit grievances. The same study also showed that people at each level of management overestimate the extent to which their subordinates feel free to express grievances, giving themselves much higher marks for accessibility than they deserve, while rating their own superiors much lower than themselves in this respect.[10]

Well-run organizations have only a small number of grievances, and management reacts to them promptly and vigorously. Most of these grievances fall into a few simple categories that are part of every manager's experience. The most common grounds for grievances are quarrels between superiors and subordinates, discrimination against an individual or a group, breaches of the organization's rules, and neglect of organizational duties.

To handle grievances, you may establish an open-door policy whereby anyone in the organization can approach you with a grievance at any time, or you may delegate an ombudsman to hear grievances on your behalf, or authorize a walking delegate to bring you grievances on behalf of the rank-and-file, or turn over all grievances to an internal tribunal. Some managers follow a closed-door policy, whereby grievances are referred back to lower levels of the organization or simply ignored. This latter policy, although widely practiced, represents the abdication rather than the exercise of managerial responsibility. The other grievance policies deserve closer attention.

The open-door policy has a good deal of rhetorical appeal and is often proudly announced by managers who would not dream of following it. Except in very small organizations, it is not an effective way to handle grievances, because the manager does not have enough time to look into the facts of each case, talk to all the people involved, and arrive at a judicious solution. Moreover, an open-door policy favors the least deserving complainants. The neurotic and self-absorbed persons who are found in every organization will not hesitate to claim the manager's ear, while more serious people will hesitate to push themselves. The manager who tries to follow an open-door policy may come to practice what Max Weber called "cadi justice," the quick, public disposition of cases by a local tyrant at the city gates. It is a hazardous role for any manager who lacks the cadi's powers of life and death.

There are two variations of the open-door policy that make it more workable. In one of these, the open door is ceremonial. The manager receives every complainant personally but refers him or her as quickly as possible to an assistant who handles the matter from then on. This procedure is fairly advantageous for complainants but not very advantageous for the manager. The situation is structured so that those who obtain satisfaction are grateful to the assistant while those who are not satisfied blame the manager.

A better variation of the open-door policy is practiced by self-confident managers who, as soon as they understand the nature of the grievance, bring in the person or persons complained about and conduct all further discussion in this conference of adversaries. But this procedure is unfair when persons high in the organization are able to take reprisals against lower-ranking persons who offend them at such a conference.

In some organizations a complainant must go to each intervening level of authority with his or her grievance before approaching the open door at the top. This looks superficially reasonable but is so drastically unfair in practice that it must be regarded as a way of repressing rather than handling grievances. It involves excessive wear and tear on the complainant and an automatic coalition of superiors against him or her.

The principal alternative to the open-door policy is a system whereby the complainant, the manager, or both are represented by competent agents during the hearing of a grievance. For example, the manager's responsibility for hearing and redressing grievances may be delegated to a committee of subordinates who are placed partly outside of the manager's control in order to assure their impartiality. From the standpoint of management, this is a nearly ideal system; such independent tribunals appear under every civilized form of government. In some organizations, however, managerial influence is so pervasive that it is difficult to assemble an impartial tribunal. Despite centuries of experience, military and naval courts-martial are not renowned for impartial justice. In other types of organization, such as industrial corporations, the rank-and-file do not have enough confidence in management to submit their grievances to a managerially appointed tribunal. The best alternative in such cases is an arbitration board composed of outsiders or including rank-and-file representatives.

Ombudsmen have recently been installed in many American organizations. The ombudsman is an autonomous representative of management assigned to hear complaints, identify justifiable grievances, and press for redress on behalf of the complainants. In the Scandinavian governments, which originated this office, the ombudsman relies only on public opinion and his powers of persuasion to get grievances redressed. A few American bureaucracies that have ombudsmen (some prisons, for example) empower them to redress certain grievances on their own authority. Under either arrangement, the ombudsman acts as a broker between the management that appoints him and the clients whose interests he is supposed to protect. The role is necessarily uncomfortable, and must be effectively insulated from the rest of the organization in order to function.

Organizations of similar type often develop quite dissimilar modes of handling grievances that seem to work about equally well, as illustrated by Steven A. Richardson's comparative study of grievance procedures on British and American merchant ships. When a British sailor has a complaint, his first step is to enlist the sympathy and support of his fellow sailors, who, as a delegation, take the complaint first to the bosun, then to the mate, and then, if it is still unsettled, to the captain. On American ships, the elected union delegate takes charge of all grievances and settles most of them by direct negotiation with the bosun, who is himself a union member. Only under unusual circumstances does the delegate go above the bosun's head to the mate or the captain.[11]

The appointment of a third party to handle grievances does not fully relieve a manager of participation in the process. You will still be involved in the grievances of your immediate subordinates, in appeals from grievance decisions at lower levels, and in the supplemental complaints inevitably generated by a grievance procedure. Whether you handle grievances directly or at second hand, there are certain principles that you should keep in mind in order to avoid the pitfalls that await you in such cases. To explain why the risk is higher for you than for your subordinates, we need to digress briefly into the theory of organization.

Every living organization has some aura of sanctity in the eyes of its members—even a bridge club or a street-corner gang. Authority exercised in the name of an organization always has a moral component. Members are expected to obey organizational directives not merely because of self-interest or coercion but also because of the goodness of the organization's purposes. Concepts of duty, loyalty, and justice seem to arise spontaneously in all organizations, regardless of the time, place, or culture in which they are set. The responsible manager of an organization is perceived by its members as the custodian of its moral force. The manager may be corrupt, lazy, incompetent, or careless without violating this ritual role, but he or she must not appear unjust.

Since subordinates lack the monarchical aura, an act of injustice by a subordinate is not likely to disturb the organization nearly as much as an unjust decision by its manager. On the other hand, the power of an organization to shape the behavior of its members is always dependent on an exchange of benefits between organizational levels. The obedience that members of organizations give to their superiors is given in direct exchange for their superiority over their own subordinates and for the equality they enjoy with their peers. When one side of this exchange is reduced, the other must decline correspondingly. Thus, the manager who undermines the legitimate authority of subordinates, or fails to defend them against the encroachment of their peers, weakens his or her own hold on them at the same time.

Most of the serious grievances that reach the top of an organization are serious precisely because they involve some dilemma between doing justice and maintaining authority. The janitor foreman fires a man for insubordination; the dismissed janitor admits that he often talked back, but points out that he never refused to do what he was told. The new choirmaster chooses a pretty young soprano as soloist for the Christmas program; she has a smaller vocal range than the older woman who has sung the part for the past five years. The tool-crib boss is demoted for failing to report an increase in pilferage; he claims that he made oral reports, which were disregarded, to the superintendent; the superintendent denies it. The crib man's story is supported by one witness, a machinist who is also his next-door neighbor.

Most grievances, of course, are more intricate than these examples, but almost all of them involve a managerial dilemma. I remember the case of a small consulting firm that paid high salaries and provided extensive fringe benefits to its employees. It had a low turnover rate and every sign of high morale even though the owner-manager traveled extensively in the conduct of the business and was often out of the office and out of the country for long periods of time. One day he hit upon the idea of rewarding his employees with a profit-sharing plan. When the plan was finally drawn up, approved by the tax authorities, and put into effect, he was startled to experience a sharp decline in his rapport with subordinates; but it was only much later, when a delegation came to him with a formal complaint, that he grasped the problem. As soon as the employees acquired an interest in profitability, they looked about for ways of keeping costs down. That reaction, of course, is one of the objectives of a profit-sharing plan. In the particular enterprise, there were relatively few costs that could be reduced by employee initiative. The largest variable category was the owner-manager's expense for travel and client entertainment. The delegation came to complain about the loss of profits chargeable to the owner-manager's customary style of doing business, and demanded, among other things, that he cease to travel first class and that he patronize cheaper restaurants. The grievance was eventually resolved, but not without permanent damage to the organization.

The rules for threading one's way through serious grievances are remarkably simple.

The first rule is to listen carefully to the original complaint. Never scold the complainant at this stage, and never, never appear to take his or her side. Then, as quickly as possible, listen to the person or persons complained about. Watch as well as listen; gestures and facial expressions are significant. Then go yourself—do not send someone else—to look at the objective evidence—the scene of the accident, the time cards for the day, the trash dumped out the window. Write down everything you hear and see. Listen to other witnesses, including, as a matter of course, all the people in intervening positions between you and the parties. Keep an open mind and make no commitments to either side until all the evidence is in.

The second rule is to follow the evidence where it leads without considering possible embarrassment to individuals or damage to the organization. This is nearly always a safer course than attempting to hush up a scandal.

The third and harshest rule is to favor a superior over a subordinate when the evidence is insufficient to decide between them. Faced with a conflict of testimony that cannot be resolved objectively, it is generally better to trust the higher-ranking witness than to reject both stories. After a fight so serious that one of the parties must leave the organization, it is usually better to dismiss the subordinate than to expel both parties. As the manager you may fancy yourself as an impartial tribunal, but organizational justice is best served in the long run by protecting organizational authority unless it has been clearly abused.

The fourth rule is to force the complainant to produce the remedy for a grievance. Indeed, he should be asked to specify the redress he wants when he makes his original complaint. (A surprising number of real grievances turn out to have no practicable remedy.) When a complaint is found to be justified, the person or persons complained against should be given an opportunity to discuss, revise, and, if possible, agree to the proposed remedy before it is put into effect.

The fifth rule is to treat similar grievances as uniformly as possible, recognizing that uneven justice is no justice at all. This means, among other things, that grievance procedures should not be secret and that any decision about a grievance should be recognized as a precedent for the settlement of future grievances of the same kind.

Outside Experts

Consultation with outside experts is another specialized form of managerial communication. These include technicians engaged for a specific task, such as surveyors or appraisers; professional advisers retained on a semipermanent basis, such as lawyers and accountants; and others who provide such managerial services as market research, supervisor training, or long-range planning.

Most of the purposes for which outside experts are hired are bona fide; their advice is often helpful and sometimes indispensable. But the outside expert is not always brought onto the organizational scene for an ostensible function.[12]

Outside experts are sometimes called in to decide a controversial issue that cannot be settled internally without hard feelings. In such a case, the fiction that the decision is based on impartial expertise helps to soften the chagrin of the losers. Even when the fiction is not entirely credible, some of the resentment provoked by the decision will be harmlessly deflected toward the outsiders.

A consultant is sometimes brought in not to discover new facts but to force facts already known upon the attention of some reluctant part of the organization. Thus, a survey of morale among the rank-and-file may be undertaken in order to compel subordinate managers to do something about problems already known to exist.

An outside expert may be called in to advise a manager to do something he has already decided to do and to provide justifications for doing it that can be displayed to various audiences inside and outside the organization. Outside experts are also likely to be retained for a number of tasks that are too painful for a manager to undertake in his own name, for example, the auditing of financial records to uncover embezzlement or a reclassification of personnel that modifies career expectations.

The outsider need not be corrupt to be malleable. The precarious character of an expert's employment makes him acutely responsive to the client's demands, expressed or unexpressed, while the client is unlikely to select a professional who does not view his problems in a sympathetic light.

The mere enumeration of these ulterior purposes suggests that consultants should be used very sparingly; they should be selected, engaged, and actively supervised by the manager to whom they report, discouraged from improvising their own liaisons with other parts of the organization, and replaced at the first intimation that they have taken a hand in the organization's internal intrigues.

An outside consultant is a managerial weapon and should not be used carelessly or left unguarded.

Consultation with the Rank-and-File

For at least fifty years, industrial psychologists and sociologists have insisted that the right way to introduce a new work process or change an old one is to consult the workers involved in the process before, during, and after the innovation in order (1) to take advantage of their realistic, firsthand knowledge of the work situation, (2) to enlist their willing cooperation, and (3) to obtain prompt feedback about the unanticipated consequences of the innovation. But although this message was enshrined in the textbooks of management, it was, for a long time, not taken seriously in American industry except in a few companies like IBM that made a fetish of involving workers in the design and redesign of work processes.[13] In most American factories and offices it continued to be assumed, in the tradition of old-fashioned scientific management, that the rank-and-file worker needed to be shown exactly what to do by somebody brighter than him- or herself and more committed to the company's goals.

Meanwhile, in faraway Japan and in some other countries like West Germany, Sweden, and South Korea, the idea of the routine ongoing participation of workers in the design of their work was being taken much more seriously and applied in all sorts of ingenious ways. At Toyota, for example, the official doctrine was:

> We believe that an individual job and the way it is performed must be activities into which are woven the original ideas of workers, not to be thought of as simply a fixed job which superiors order one to perform.[14]

By the beginning of the 1980s this philosophy and some of the other personnel practices associated with it, like lifetime employment security for blue-collar workers, had given the Japanese a commanding lead over the United States in the manufacture of automobiles, steel, audiovisual equipment, microprocessors, and promised to give them a margin of advantage in any other field of production where they might choose to concentrate their efforts. Other countries too seem to be able to turn out better and cheaper manufactured products than the United States although our industrial superiority to the rest of the world had been taken for granted throughout most of the twentieth century. The gradual revelation of Japanese superiority in manufacturing sent American managers flocking in droves to companies in Tokyo and Osaka to study their secrets. General Motors and Ford both introduced massive Quality Circle programs in 1980 that were directly patterned upon Japanese models. Nevertheless, despite all this fanfare, the idea of consulting the rank-and-file still comes hard to the managers of large private enterprises in the United States and the practice is virtually unknown in government agencies and other public enterprises.

Although there are features of Japanese management methods that are peculiar to Japanese culture, the necessity of consulting the workers about how they ought to do their work is so obvious and elementary that the failure to do it must be taken as a pathological form of irresponsibility. Only the people on the ground know where the bodies are buried. In the telephone company that I studied just before Quality Circles became the fashion in the telephone industry, we introduced something similar called "Upward Planning" to remedy certain operational defects, such as the inability of the business office to reach the repair service by telephone and the habit of assigning the same telephone number to two or three different customers at the same time. When planning teams composed of reception clerks, telephone operators, linemen, repairmen, and others directly involved were brought together to plan organizational improvements to cure these problems, the procedure worked beautifully. The form of consultation with the rank-and-file is not that important: what matters is that they be continuously consulted and that their informed judgments be taken into account.

After Consultation

Just as consultation should precede nearly every managerial decision, the diffusion of information ought to follow every decision as a matter of course. The minimum requirement is that everyone consulted about the decision should be fully informed as soon as it has been made. This principle, although self-evident, is often violated by managers in a hurry or obsessed with secrecy, almost always to their own disadvantage.

The general problem of whom to inform about what is shared by everyone from the top to the bottom of every organization, and nearly all of these people occasionally tell some people what they shouldn't know or fail to tell them what they should know. Errors of the first kind usually have trivial consequences for the organization, although they may be serious for individuals. The error of not telling people what they need to know is much more troublesome for the organization because it leads both to inappropriate behavior and hurt feelings. The father of the infant princess who later became the Sleeping Beauty invited all the fairies in his kingdom to the christening feast, but according to the old tale he forgot one important fairy, who was so furious at the slight that she canceled out the other fairies' blessings by putting a curse on the child. This sort of thing happens in large organizations every day, when people who are entitled to be informed about some matter are carelessly overlooked.

The manager, as I said before, shares this problem with everyone else; but his failures to diffuse information have greater effect, partly because he has more information to diffuse, partly because insults from him, like courtesies from him, carry unusual weight. There is no way to avoid errors of omission completely, but their occurrence can be greatly reduced by constant effort and by using checklists of names.

It is nearly impossible for someone at the top of an organization to understand how little of the organization is visible to people at lower levels. It is not uncommon for employee surveys to turn up employees who cannot correctly identify their own supervisors, the departments in which they work, or the nature of the enterprise.

In a study I conducted many years ago, we found that the majority of officers in an air force division were unfamiliar with the missions of their own units as set down in the organization's manual. The majority of enlisted men could not identify their own jobs and had only an approximate idea of their own duties. Neither junior officers nor enlisted personnel had any clear picture of the division's structure or understood its relationship to the military and civilian agencies with which it had routine contact. The commanding general of the division, an officer famous for his solid achievements and his flamboyant style, found some of these results incredible. "They couldn't not know their own squadron commanders," he objected, "any more than not know me." The next survey of the division's personnel asked them to identify their commanding general; a sizable percentage had never heard of him.

People in organizations must not be expected to acquire a standard inventory of information by osmosis. They need to have it systematically communicated to them by means of orientation sessions, written materials circulated for study, posted signs, public assemblies, newsletters, and other devices. What is meant to be remembered must then be frequently repeated. Internal orientation is a continuous activity in any well-run organization.

Secrecy and Security

Every organization has some need for secrecy. Generally speaking, poor managers try to keep as many secrets as possible, while good managers try to have as few secrets as possible.

The attempt to guard a large amount of information is intrinsically self-defeating. A large stock of secrets requires a large number of custodians and the frequent deposit and withdrawal of confidential documents. Since it is unlikely that all custodians can be trusted or that adequate surveillance of a large traffic in secret materials can be maintained, the effort to keep many secrets makes it difficult to protect the few secrets that really matter. In organizations already plagued by excessive secrecy, there is usually some effort made to identify the real secrets by special labels like "Top Secret" or "For Eyes Only," and by ritual devices like burnbags and coding machines. On balance, these probably make the real secrets more vulnerable by flagging them so clearly.

Once introduced into an organization, security classification spreads like a fungus, for obvious reasons. The right to keep organizational secrets is always a mark of organizational status—symbolically, because it signifies that the organization trusts the keeper; practically, because secret information gives the keeper a tactical advantage in the conduct of his or her own affairs. Since security classifications are among the cheapest of all status symbols, they are likely to be overproduced. The effects of such overproduction are long lasting, for the security label attached to trivial or outdated information makes declassification difficult. The U.S. government, a notable victim of this blight, stores thousands of tons of unimportant documents that cannot be easily inspected or thrown away because of their security labels.

Secrecy is costly for an organization in many other ways. It slows down important communications and interferes with routine ones, it creates pockets of ignorance at points where knowledge is needed, and it serves to conceal fraud, malfeasance, and sabotage. The availability of a cloak of secrecy always seems to encourage wrongdoing by organizational functionaries. On the one hand, they can justify wrongdoing by the excuse of security. On the other hand, a security cover makes it difficult to distinguish between normal and abnormal conduct.

As Edmond Cahn has suggested, the manager who takes a secret action ought to ask himself such questions as: How would the public view the action if all the facts were revealed? How would you characterize the action if it had been done by your worst enemy?[15]

Managerial secrecy ought, ideally, to be restricted to those few items of information whose revelation would damage the organization, but not expose it to any shame. Most of the information that answers this description falls into three categories: (1) plans of action that would be hampered or prevented if prematurely exposed, such as battle plans, site acquisition plans, merger plans, and campaign plans; (2) knowledge that is useful to the organization by virtue of being unknown to outsiders, such as secret product formulas; or (3) information about persons, collected by the organization for proper purposes, which might cause embarrassment or suffering if made public, such as performance ratings and disciplinary records.

Some other types of information are kept secret by organizations primarily to entertain their members. The remarkable Seven Society at the University of Virginia is known to make donations to college projects and to issue occasional statements on college issues. Everything else about the society is secret, with the sole exception that at a member's death the fact of his having belonged to the society is finally made public. Secrecy of this kind is a game played for its own sake. Similar games are played for political, religious, social, and criminal purposes. The manager of a secret society has some unique problems, but they have not been empirically studied and will not be discussed here. Ordinary organizations operate better with minimum secrecy, and the manager who systematically attempts to reduce the number of locked files and confidential stamps in his or her organization will be amazed to discover how much sensitive information becomes harmless when exposed to the light of day.

The methods of keeping a real secret, of course, remain what they have always been. Tell it sparingly and only to people who have an unmistakable need to know. Make the fewest possible documents and conceal them unobtrusively. Trust no strangers.

Spies and Agents

The communication network of every organization, large or small, has a seamy underside for the circulation of stolen information and misinformation. Many organizations can expect professional spies to be sent in from outside. Nearly every organization has amateur spies who snoop for fun and profit. In nearly all organizations there is some circulation of false or grossly exaggerated rumors.

On the large scene of public affairs, spying has been practiced throughout history, but for every general or statesman who has known how to make good use of spies, another has been led to ruin by them. Without the blundering of their own spies, the British might have put down the American Revolution. General McClellan could probably have won the Civil War for the Union in 1862 had he not relied upon the reports of Confederate strength obtained for him at great expense by the Pinkertons. The Vietnam disaster could not have begun or been continued by the United States without the assistance of unreliable spies. Without their secret agents, Mary, Queen of Scots, might have died in bed; Napoleon might have retained his crown; and President Nixon might have occupied a distinguished place in American history.

The little that is publicly known about industrial and commercial espionage suggests that these forms of spying, too, are often more damaging to their users than to their intended victims.

Aside from the obvious risks—betrayal by double agents, exposure of one's own plans, being lured by the other side into acting on false information—there is the overriding risk that the information provided by spies will be biased in favor of their continued employment. They are inclined to suppress information that casts doubt upon their earlier reports or that is inconsistent with the picture of the situation they have built up. This bias often sets the stage for disaster.

Nevertheless, there are some managerial occasions that do call for spying inside or outside the organization; for example, an adversary is known to be deploying a secret weapon and it is essential to have more information about it, or a conspiracy is brewing in the organization and one of the conspirators is willing to reveal it. Note, however, that the first of these problems might be better handled by scouting than by spying, while the second needs a voluntary informant rather than a spy. The secret agent planted somewhere to report regularly may become either an agent provocateur who fabricates conspiracies in order to betray them, or a real conspirator who lulls his or her employer with false information. The scout sent out from one's own ranks and the voluntary informant who reveals a plot have much more to lose than to gain if their information turns out to be false. A spy who might safely provide false information should never be trusted as far as the door.

Grapevines

It is usually possible for a manager to find out something about how rumors circulate in his or her organization and, within limits, to adapt the process to the organization's advantage.

A classic experiment, first developed by Gordon Allport, is often staged in social psychology classrooms to show how information is distorted in the transmittal of a rumor.[16] A student chosen at random from the class is handed a picture with a number of complicated details—for example, a summer street scene in a large city showing an ice-cream vendor surrounded by several children in the foreground, two dogs being walked on leashes nearby, and a firehouse in the background. The first student is asked to whisper a description of the picture to her neighbor who, in turn, whispers as much as he can remember to his neighbor, and so on through fifteen or twenty persons. After each subject has whispered his or her version, he or she writes it down so that changes in the form and content of the message can be traced from the beginning to the end of the chain. The changes that occur are startling and ludicrous. The message that emerged at the end of one such chain, based on the picture described above, was: "The picture shows a burning barn. About fifty horses have been led out of the barn. Some of them are running away."

If we look at the intermediate versions, we find that most of the distortion occurred at the beginning of the chain when the firehouse became a fire, the dogs turned into horses, and the ice-cream vendor disappeared. Later on the description assumed the tripartite form characteristic of folk tales; exaggeration took place—*two* horses became *some* horses, which became *many* horses, which became *fifty* horses—and new elements were invented to fill the logical gaps created by previous distortions. The barn, for example, appeared suddenly as a link between "fire" and "horses." Toward the end of the chain, the story was so condensed and simplified that it could be transmitted from person to person without appreciable distortion.

This process of distortion can often be observed in demoralized organizations, but it is not characteristic of normally functioning organizations. Field studies of rumors in armies, political parties, factories, hospitals, and prisons have found that most of the rumors that circulate in well-integrated organizations carry substantially accurate information, flow through fairly reliable channels, and are subject to multiple cross-checks that discourage distortions. This kind of communication network is often called a grapevine. In a well-integrated organization, the grapevine is usually reliable.

Generally speaking, an effective grapevine ought to be considered as an organizational asset, partly because it supplements formal channels of communications, and partly because it suppresses unfounded rumors and other kinds of misinformation.

A grapevine is capable of transmitting a variety of messages on a variety of topics. What it actually transmits during a given period seems to depend on the supply of, and demand for, particular kinds of information. The grapevine is most active when information is scarce and the demand for it is high; it is least active when the information is plentiful and the demand for it is low. If an organization's future plans are kept secret, there will be many rumors about future plans. If the plans are widely publicized, there will be few such rumors and perhaps none at all. Some sorts of information, like scandalous gossip, are always in demand and usually in short supply. When information in this category becomes available, the grapevine transmits it far and wide.

But an organization's demand for information of a particular type can be satiated by oversupplying information even though it is not the precise information demanded. Once in an invasion convoy, the captain of a ship on which I traveled announced over the ship's loudspeakers every bit of interesting information that came to the bridge, such as a submarine search by escort vessels or a change in the weather at the invasion site. There were many uncertainties in the impending operation, but the frequent announcements so satiated the demand for information that, although the unit to which I belonged had a hyperactive grapevine, it circulated no rumors of any kind until we had disembarked from the ship. The only dependable method of silencing a grapevine is to supply it with more information than it wants on topics that are related to the information that is being withheld.

A somewhat dubious method of using a grapevine for managerial purposes is to feed information into it at strategic points, for example, by exposing confidential papers to known rumormongers. The information may be important but not suitable for official dissemination, as in the case of a merger negotiation that has not yet reached the stage at which an announcement is possible.

Repairing Broken Links

One of the most common problems encountered by managers is the breakdown of communication between two positions that are closely connected in the table of organization and are supposed to interact routinely. The incumbents may have a personal quarrel, may differ about the purposes of a program for which they share responsibility, may be unable to settle a dispute about authority, or may be unwilling to work together for various other reasons. I once knew a manufacturing company that had only two vice-presidents, one for marketing and one for production. Although they worked in the same building, they did not exchange a single word for several years. Like governments that do not recognize each other and have to communicate through a neutral power, these executives used the president of the company as their intermediary for essential messages.

Communication breakdowns occur at every organizational level and for all sorts of reasons. In the foregoing case, the production vice-president, trained in an advanced branch of engineering, regarded the marketing vice-president as a charlatan bent on degrading the company's solid and reliable products by cheap sales gimmicks and sensational advertising. He hated him with a consuming passion. The marketing vice-president had no strong feelings about his colleague but regarded him as dull and stubborn. The president, an engineer with a flair for marketing, respected and liked both men and never understood why he found it so difficult to bring them together. When, at long last, he made a determined effort to do so, the marketing vice-president resigned and left the company.

Breaks in communication occur at all organizational levels, but the manager is most likely to be aware of being directly involved when he finds himself avoiding, or being avoided by, a subordinate.

Although it is often possible to short-circuit a break in communication so that the organizational program goes on without apparent disturbance, every such break promises trouble sooner or later and should be repaired if possible. The conventional method of repairing a break is to bring the parties together in the presence of their common superior for an airing of mutual grievances. Once in a while, when the antagonism or fear that keeps the parties apart derives from a misunderstanding, this method actually works. An alternative is to "knock their heads together," threatening both parties with dire penalties unless they make some effort to resolve their differences. When both methods fail, you, the manager, will find yourself confronted with what appears to be a clash of incompatible personalities and you will be tempted to interpret the behavior of one or both parties as neurotic. This interpretation will be especially plausible if your "head-knocking" has put the parties under such psychological strain that they are indeed behaving abnormally, but it is not a helpful guide to further action. Digging a little deeper, you will discover that in addition to their supposed incompatibility, the people who refuse to communicate have substantial differences of interest imposed upon them by their positions in the organizational structure, so that at least one of them cannot interact freely with the other without jeopardizing his or her own interests or those of a faction he or she represents. Surprisingly often, the clash of interests is due to some indecision of the manager.

In the case described above, the breach between the two vice-presidents reflected the president's inability to choose between a conservative and an innovative marketing policy. This indecision encouraged his subordinates to pursue incompatible goals. The president flattered himself that he was promoting a kind of Hegelian synthesis of opposing ideas—he once compared his role to that of an orchestra conductor balancing the strings against the woodwinds—but rather than orchestrating the two vice-presidents, he inflamed their mutual distrust by instructing them to follow inconsistent versions of marketing policy. The important thing that happened when he brought them together to settle their differences was that he discovered which policy he really preferred and reorganized the company accordingly.

The trick of repairing a break in communication is to start with the assumption that the problem is attributable to a managerial error of some kind, and to search for that error. Sometimes, as in the case cited above, the manager who resolves his own indecision will no longer be able to present himself as an impartial arbiter but will throw his weight behind one of the parties, leaving the other party no choice but to get out. But it may also happen that the loser in a decision of this kind welcomes the resolution of ambiguity nearly as much as the winner and finds he can live comfortably with the decision. Whether the adjustment is smooth or not, the organization is usually better off after the break has been repaired.

Once in a long while the most careful scrutiny of a break in communication between two persons who are supposed to cooperate will not uncover any managerial error, but simply some brew of jealousy, irascibility, ethnic prejudice, or private grudge. In such cases, the old formula for conciliation outlined in the *Book of Common Prayer* is a good procedure to follow, making it clear to those concerned that if they insist on pursuing their private feuds they will be expelled from the organization:

> The same order shall the Minister use with those, betwixt whom he perceiveth malice and hatred to reign; not suffering them to be partakers of the Lord's Table, until he know them to be reconciled. And if one of the parties, so at variance, be content to forgive from the bottom of his heart all that the other has trespassed against him, and to make amends for that wherein he himself hath offended, and the other party will not be persuaded to a godly unity, but remain still in his frowardness and malice; the Minister in that case ought to admit the penitent person to the Holy Communion and not him that is obstinate.

An entirely different way of repairing breaks in communication between organizational positions is to shift people around until they sort themselves into compatible pairs. Daniel Katz provides the following illustration:

> When Studebaker introduced a new assembly line years ago, there was conflict between union and management over what the new rates should be. The problem was handled by simply rotating all the foremen and stewards on the new line until they got a foreman-steward combination that could agree on the rates that should be set.[17]

Nonverbal Communication

Nonverbal messages often contain more information than verbal messages, and nonverbal communication by managers is particularly effective. Since you are more closely observed than other members of the organization, the messages implicit in your gestures, displays, and actions are more effectively transmitted. Because you have more freedom of movement within the organization's territory and more autonomy in arranging the personal space around you, you have, in effect, a larger nonverbal vocabulary than other people. Your responsibility for conducting organizational rituals requires others to imitate you, and you can also specify gestures, displays, and actions in which you may not be imitated.

This last sounds more abstruse than it is. In most organizations, the manager's salary cannot be matched or exceeded by any other salary; hence, the manager who sets his own salary imposes an upper limit on all salaries paid by the organization. The size and furnishings of your office, the cost of your official car, the length of your vacation, and the extent of your outside affiliations are all likely to have the similar effect of setting limits to the pretensions of your subordinates. You are always, in some ways, what David Riesman calls a "Captain of Consumption."[18]

It is almost impossible to enumerate all the ways in which nonverbal messages can be conveyed, but the most important media include spatial arrangements, movements from one place to another, appearances and nonappearances at ceremonies, allotments of time, security measures, sociability patterns, personal gestures, and costumes. The variety of these media make nonverbal communication highly entertaining for those involved, but there is always some danger of being misunderstood or of showing more than one wants to tell. It would be laborious to look at each type of nonverbal expression separately, but we can get a pretty good idea of how they work by examining a few types from the standpoint of the manager who understands their possibilities—for example, (1) the microgeography of office buildings, (2) expressive movements in conferences, and (3) the control of behavior by example.

The Microgeography of Office Buildings

Microgeography is the study of the space surrounding individuals and small groups. The microgeography of an office building includes its physical structure, floor plans, the location of people and facilities, and the flow of internal traffic.

The physical structure of a building affects any social system housed within it. Tall buildings favor hierarchical relations, but interfere with lateral communications among related departments. Low flat buildings have the opposite effect. A building with a single main entrance encourages a sense of organizational identity; a building with multiple entrances discourages it.

Consider a twelve-story structure that houses the headquarters of a single organization. If the manager's office is placed on the top floor—as it is likely to be, for the advantages of quiet, privacy, and view—the entire building will tend to fall into a hierarchical pattern with the status of individuals and departments measured by their distance from the top. The top floor will take on a hushed, unearthly atmosphere and access to it will be heavily guarded by elevator operators and receptionists. The next two or three floors will imitate the luxury and exclusiveness of the top floor as far as their means allow. Fantastic rumors about "life at the top" will circulate in the lower depths and the occupants of the top floors will be too isolated to supervise lower-floor activities effectively.

If the offices of the manager and his principal assistants are located on the ground floor, location on higher floors will have no automatic significance and the isolation of top management from the organization will be avoided. But some of the departments located on upper floors will become independent mountain kingdoms, jealous of their autonomy and inaccessible to people from other parts of the building.

In order to get the widest control, the manager's office should be placed in the middle part of the building, but the top floor should be reserved for such facilities as conference rooms, lounges, an executive dining room, or the library. Such a pattern stretches both managerial and rank-and-file traffic along the whole height of the building and discourages the development of isolated enclaves. It permits you to see your subordinates in their own offices as often, or more often, than you invite them to your own. It also enables you and your staff to move about the building in your daily routines and to inspect an organizational activity without creating a disturbance.

This sort of thing is elementary, although often neglected in architectural design. A much more complicated microgeographical problem is how to locate all the parts of an organization in a building without unintentionally creating barriers that interfere with essential work, or creating channels of access that encourage illicit activities.

One early microgeographical study described a group of file clerks who, without any particular intention, had been put into an alcove in a very large office. Their file cabinets partly blocked the entrance to the alcove and a fire door gave them private access to a rear corridor. In a relatively short time, the clerks assigned to the alcove became a privileged and cohesive elite who held themselves aloof from the canaille in the outer office, ignoring their supervisor and running their affairs to suit themselves. When, eventually, they were taken out of the alcove and placed elsewhere in the large office, they fortified themselves within a new and larger wall of file cabinets and resisted the reduction of their privileges with astonishing ferocity. The problem was not resolved until nearly all the members of the original group had been replaced.

Generally speaking, a physical barrier between two groups of people in an organization can be counted on to create a social barrier and to confer a status advantage on whoever controls passage through the barrier. Where there is no barrier at all to mark a division between groups, as when the secretaries of unrelated departments are placed in the same stenographic pool, there is likely to be a much freer flow of information than the organization intends.

Similarly, any accidental difference in physical facilities is almost certain to create status differences. In a modern high-rise building with both outside and inside offices, an outside office will confer prestige and a corner outside office with windows on two sides will give its occupant a margin of superiority over all the people in outside offices along the same corridor. If one corner office is larger than the others, it will identify its occupant as superior to everyone else on the floor, and if that does not correspond to the table of organization, there is bound to be trouble. If all the offices on a floor are of identical size, the occupants of corner offices will be privileged, but isolated from each other. If the building is redesigned to eliminate all corner offices but one, making storerooms out of the other three corners, proximity to the remaining corner office may become so important a mark of status that every new arrival or departure causes an agonizing round of musical chairs.

The matching of rooms, corridors, distances, and lines of sight to an intended pattern of organizational relationships is an unending jigsaw puzzle. In a large organization it can never be completely solved, but approximate solutions can be imposed by careful planning or found by trial and error.

Expressive Movements in Conferences

The study of expressive movements—body placement, gestures, and other body signs—ought to be practiced by every manager of an organization. Excluded from full participation in the grapevine and with little information about the private sentiments of subordinates, you must often rely on your unaided observation to discover what everybody else in the organization already knows. On the other hand, you have exceptional opportunities for observation because you see so many people and are able to choose the setting in which you will see them.

Consider the opportunities for observation in the routine conference a manager might hold with six or seven subordinates. The order of arrival is significant. Early arrival generally signifies eagerness to participate, and lateness or absence usually indicates some reluctance connected with the business at hand, or some mistrust of the other participants. People who arrive together and deep in conversation are either announcing a coalition or concealing a quarrel.

The selection of seats is significant (Figure 5). Even in a meeting with fixed seating arrangements, small variations—a place skipped, a chair shoved to one side or the other—are significant. People who crowd close to the chairman are likely to be seeking his or her support. Those who isolate themselves at the other end of the table may be girding for battle. A real fight, as distinct from a difference of opinion, usually aligns people into visible factions. Positions at the end of a long table or in the middle of a side table are taken by people who intend to participate actively, while the corners are occupied by those who want to remain inconspicuous.[19]

Over a period of some years I attended business conferences in a

Figure 5

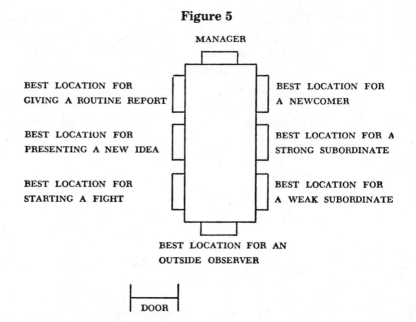

MANAGER

BEST LOCATION FOR
GIVING A ROUTINE REPORT

BEST LOCATION FOR
A NEWCOMER

BEST LOCATION FOR
PRESENTING A NEW IDEA

BEST LOCATION FOR A
STRONG SUBORDINATE

BEST LOCATION FOR
STARTING A FIGHT

BEST LOCATION FOR
A WEAK SUBORDINATE

BEST LOCATION FOR AN
OUTSIDE OBSERVER

DOOR

room with an oval table and an equal number of black chairs and white chairs. There was a feeble standing joke about the good guys sitting in white chairs and the bad guys in black chairs but, joke or not, several odd little customs developed out of the necessity for each participant to choose a black or a white chair at the beginning of each meeting. The white chairs came to be associated with optimism, growth, and good news; the black chairs with disapproval, reorganization, and financial stringency. In this way, participants signaled in advance the general tone of their contribution to a particular meeting. People on the same side of a controversial issue were likely to choose like-colored chairs. The occasional efforts of individuals to adopt one color or the other permanently and thus avoid the choice were detected by the other participants and subjected to the kind of pointed joking by which violations of etiquette are corrected.

Expressive movements such as gestures, smiles and frowns, the placement of arms and legs, seated posture, fiddling and doodling, scratching and yawning, crossed glances, looking toward or away from a speaker, tones of voice, and the length and character of silences, serve in any meeting to amplify and clarify what is said and may indeed be more informative than any of the words spoken. The first thing for you to do as manager in a conference is to look and to listen. If these demanding activities keep you from talking as much as you would like, so much the better.

Behavior Control by Example

The norms of any organization consist largely of informal expectations and unstated rules. As manager, and as keeper of the collective conscience, you have more power to modify informal norms and to enact new ones than you have with respect to the organization's written rules and regulations. This power is most readily exercised over the norms that say what a member owes to the organization and what he or she may legitimately take from it.

In an enterprise with regular working hours, say 9:00 to 5:00 with lunch from 12:00 to 1:00, your working schedule is likely to determine what hours are kept by all the people who do not punch time clocks and by some of those who do. If it is your habit to come in about 10:30, be out to lunch from 12:00 to 2:00, and leave the office around 4:00, your higher-ranking subordinates will probably come to work after 9:00 and leave before 5:00, spacing their comings and goings so that they are present when you arrive and when you leave. Their lunches will certainly average more than an hour. Their subordinates, in turn, will time themselves in a similar fashion. These departures from the working schedule will sacrifice hundreds or thousands of working hours without any compensating benefit, but with some damage to the self-esteem of the executives who cheat a little on their hours, and to the morale of the rank-and-file workers who are compelled to arrive and leave on time. No amount of exhortation will make much difference, but you, the manager, can change the situation overnight by coming in at 9:00, lunching from 12:00 to 1:00, and leaving at 5:00. Within a week, most of the organization will be on that schedule and will remain on it as long as you do.

If you choose to come in at 8:00 and to leave at 6:00, the effect will be less salutary. By following the official schedule, you create an expectation that everybody else will do so. When you exceed it, you do not create any clear expectation for others (except perhaps for your personal assistants) but merely identify yourself as a fanatical worker. This will certainly have some influence on the time schedule of other members of the organization, but all that can be reliably predicted is that they will put in longer hours than if you come in late and leave early.

As manager, you can usually enforce any sumptuary rule you are willing to follow yourself. If you log your personal telephone calls and reimburse the organization for them, you will find it fairly easy to prevent other people from charging personal calls to the organization; otherwise, the practice may be irrepressible.

If you travel economy class, no one in the organization is likely to buy first-class tickets; it will not even be necessary to formulate a rule. If you have a small, inexpensive official car, no one else in the organization will feel entitled to a limousine; if you have a limousine with a chauffeur, you will sooner or later have to concede either part-time limousines or unchauffeured luxury cars to your principal subordinates.

Corporation or union or government executives who dazzle their subordinates with jet planes and fast boats, rosewood desks and office tapestries, and official trips to the Riviera may think they read admiration in their subordinates' eyes; what they really see is a glint of matching greed.

How to Recognize Effective Communication

The volume of communication and the degree of consensus required differ from one type of organization to another, but if and when you achieve effective communication, you will observe that:

1. The routine operational reports that reach you are seldom late and never falsified.

2. When you ask for a special report on some phase of the organizational program, you are never told that the information exists but cannot be assembled without excessive trouble or expense.

3. Your own formulations of organizational policies and problems are often repeated back to you by other people.

4. You seldom find yourself in disagreement with the priorities assigned to problems by your subordinates.

5. You are usually comfortable at meetings and conferences within the organization, whether you preside or attend as a visitor.

6. When you engage in consultation about a problem, you invariably learn new and important things, but they are not the kind of new things that make you change your whole picture of the organization.

7. When you make an important decision, the grapevine carries the news throughout the organization before an official announcement can be made.

8. The public speeches and actions of your subordinates seldom embarrass you.

9. Your subordinates often suggest a plan you have been turning over in your mind, or install a new procedure you have been about to suggest.

10. There are many things going on in the organization that you know nothing about, but they do not make you apprehensive.

11. The relatively few grievances that come to you can be promptly and vigorously handled without disrupting the organization.

12. You have very few secrets, and those you have can be safely confided to your close associates.

13. You have no regular talebearers at lower levels of the organization, and do not want any.

14. There is no part of the organization from which you cannot obtain routine communications or which fail to respond to your routine communications.

15. Misunderstandings and mistakes in communication between yourself and various parts of the organization occur quite frequently, but do not stay undetected.

CHAPTER THREE

Productivity

The bottleneck is at the top of the bottle.
An Old Saying

Efficiency and Effectiveness

Every organization has work to do in the real world and some way of measuring how well that work is done. The responsibility of a manager is to see that the work gets done as efficiently and effectively as possible, whether it consists of producing goods, winning games, teaching pupils, preventing crimes, defending a frontier, making scientific discoveries, staging an entertainment, or any of the myriad other tasks that organizations undertake. The devices that measure efficiency and effectiveness are as diverse as the tasks themselves, but are inescapable; the manager must accept the conventional yardsticks, whatever they are. If the organization is a retail store, you cannot decide to disregard profitability; if it is a professional baseball team, you cannot replace the number of games won and lost with some other measure of performance more to your liking. You can, and often will, introduce additional measures of performance to move the organizational program in one direction or another, but these will not count unless the conventional yardsticks are satisfied at the same time.

The conventional yardsticks of performance cover both efficiency and effectiveness. An organization is *efficient* if, among similar organizations, its output is relatively high in relation to its input. It is *effective* if it achieves its intended goals. An organization may be efficient without being effective. Some declining businesses are models of operating efficiency. An organization may be effective without being especially efficient. Victorious armies can be very wasteful. Efficiency and effectiveness are closely related but they are not interchangeable.

Although efficiency and effectiveness are both important, effectiveness is more important. In the numerous situations that require a choice between them, it is generally advisable to make some sacrifice of efficiency for the sake of effectiveness, provided that your organization's survival is not thereby jeopardized. Most good managers grasp this principle intuitively, but it is helpful, even for them, to understand the reasons for it.

The Organization as a Quasi-Machine

Every human organization can be described as if it were a machine. It is designed for a particular purpose and composed of specialized moving parts. It absorbs energy and materials and converts them into other forms. It requires both routine maintenance and emergency repairs. From time to time some critical part breaks down and the organization ceases to function until the broken part is repaired or replaced.

In some other ways, an organization is spectacularly unlike a machine. Its specialized moving parts—people—are incapable of behaving in a fully mechanical way even on an assembly line or in a marching band. The human parts of an organization never do exactly what the organization wants them to do. Each of them has purposes of his or her own that are incongruent with those of the organization, and each of them participates in the organizational program in an intermittent and individual way.

The subgroups that compose an organization are similarly unreliable. They, too, have goals that are inconsistent with those of the whole organization. Nearly every department and section, for example, seeks to enhance its own importance, even when that involves a loss of efficiency or effectiveness for the whole organization.

To put it as plainly as possible, the human organization, as a quasi-machine, seldom runs as smoothly as a real machine in good working order. At any given time, some of the quasi-machine's parts are practicing what Thorstein Veblen called "the conscientious withdrawal of efficiency," and other parts are engaged in sabotage, an old French word that originally meant trampling on the product of one's labor with wooden shoes.

On the other hand, no real machine is as effective as a quasi-machine for the accomplishment of tasks under changing conditions. Being human, the quasi-machine can restructure itself as it goes along. The individual parts of which it is composed develop new functions on their own initiative. The interaction between them may lead to coordinated efforts of great subtlety and power.

The operator of a quasi-machine has two recurrent problems: how to keep the thing from falling apart and how to get more work out of it than it is supposedly capable of. What you do to solve these problems is called supervision in some organizations and leadership in others, the latter term being generally preferred in organizations that cannot be certain of achieving their goals, such as armies and orchestras. Because of that uncertainty and the excitement it produces, a great deal of attention is concentrated on the individual at the top, who, regardless of personal characteristics, assumes, if successful, the charisma that seems to separate leadership from mere supervision. "I have observed," writes David Ogilvy, "that no creative organization, whether it is a research laboratory, a magazine, a Paris kitchen, or an advertising agency, will produce a great body of work unless it is led by a *formidable* individual."[1] But formidable or not, a charismatic leader, like any other responsible manager, gets the work out by supervising people.

Direct and Indirect Supervision

There are two general modes of supervision: direct and indirect. They are governed by different principles. Many managerial positions require a continual shuttling between these modes. In theory, direct supervision presents fewer problems than indirect supervision since it is less dependent upon third parties. In practice, direct supervision requires more concentration and longer practice, and is easier to botch.

The Principles of Direct Supervision

1. *Set unmistakable goals.* The first step in getting any kind of work done under direct supervision is to make clear what the work is for, why it needs to be done in a particular way, and what constitutes suc-

cess in its performance. Even in the most elementary collective tasks, it is rash to assume that either the purposes of the task or the desired standards of performance are too obvious to require explanation. In almost every successful performance of a group task, goals and standards must be set in advance, clearly communicated, kept constantly in view, and dramatized along the way.

Goal-setting is easiest in elite organizations—the great research laboratory, the three-star restaurant kitchen, the world-renowned orchestra, the champion athletic team—where maximum excellence is sought and everyone expects the leader to demand infinite pains for the sake of excellence. Goal-setting is more difficult in mediocre organizations, and it is often useful to concentrate on one aspect of the work for the sake of overall improvement. I knew a man who ran the typing pool in a large engineering firm and supervised a dozen typists who turned out endless pages of reports and specifications. One day, he was moved by the sight of several typists using their erasers at the same time to announce that from then on he would demand perfect, error-free typing. Corrections and erasures would no longer be permitted. Erasers were to be thrown away. The typist who made a mistake of any kind was to discard that page and start again. The first few days of the new system were marked by tears, protests, and a great waste of paper. Thereafter, the error rate declined to a negligible level and stayed there as long as that supervisor remained in charge and was able to explain to each new recruit that the goal was perfect, error-free typing.

2. *Supervise the work more than the worker.* The essence of supervised work is that whatever the worker produces comes to the attention of the supervisor, so that every improvement or deterioration in the quality of work (or in the quality of supervision) is noticed and stimulates appropriate feedback. The chef who sits at the kitchen door and tastes every dish as it passes, the office manager who scans every typed page before it goes out, the farmer who looks at the new bales of hay and counts them and checks over the mowing machine and the baler at the end of the day, all find it easy to communicate with their workers.

Supervising the worker is another matter entirely. The unnecessary exercise of personal authority is a kind of sabotage endlessly practiced by incompetent supervisors. Most people need a zone of freedom around them in order to work well. It is hard to find anyone, no matter how meek or discouraged, who willingly submits to tighter control than the necessities of the work require.

3. *Distinguish between essential and nonessential rules.* There is an old textbook distinction in sociology between *folkways,* which are social practices, and *mores,* which are the rules that hold a society together. Every work group has its own folkways and mores, and the supervisor is responsible for keeping them distinct. If you are clear in your own mind about which rules are essential and which are not, you are not likely to fritter away your authority in efforts to get perfect compliance with rules such as "No Smoking" or "All tools must be returned to the tool crib by the end of the day."*

But with respect to those few norms that express the organization's moral commitments and do call for perfect compliance, the supervisor's best course is to treat every violation as harshly as his or her powers allow. Ogilvy provides this edifying example from his experience in the kitchen of a great French restaurant:

> Soon after I joined M. Pitard's brigade, I was faced with a problem of morality for which neither my father nor my schoolmasters had prepared me. The *chef garde-manger* sent me to the *chef saucier* with some raw sweetbreads which smelled so putrid that I knew they would endanger the life of any client who ate them; the sauce would mask their condition, and the client would eat them. I protested to the *chef garde-manger,* but he told me to carry out his order; he knew that he would be in hot water if M. Pitard discovered that he had run out of fresh sweetbreads. What was I to do? I had been brought up to believe that it was dishonorable to inform. But I did just that. I took the putrid sweetbreads to M. Pitard and invited him to smell them. He did so and, without a word to me, went over to the *chef garde-manger* and fired him on the spot. This poor bastard had to leave, then and there.[2]

4. *Reward sparingly; punish much more sparingly.* The usual form of reward in work groups is praise. The usual form of punishment is criticism. Public praise or public criticism have much higher intensity, of course, than praise or criticism in private. Other forms of reward and punishment are raises and pay reductions, bonuses and fines, promotions and demotions, the extension and withdrawal of privileges.

It can usually be observed in an organized group that the aversion to a given punishment is greater than the desire for an equivalent reward. This can be demonstrated with laboratory precision by anyone who controls a payroll. Step 1: Raise everybody's wages by 10

---

*If for some special reason it *is* essential to repress smoking or get all tools returned to the tool crib, the problem must be approached less authoritatively—for example, by calling all those concerned together to develop an enforcement plan.

percent. The effect on productivity and morale will be nearly imperceptible. Step 2: After an interval of weeks or months, lower the same wages by 5 percent. The effect on productivity and morale will be disastrous.

All sorts of variations on this unwise experiment can be devised. For example, raising the wages of part of a work group can be counted on to demoralize those who are not raised. A reduction of pay or privileges amounts to a reduction in the ability of the workers to obtain satisfaction through the organization and, inasmuch as they prefer satisfaction to frustration, they are bound to resist. But individuals in organized groups seldom evaluate their pay and privileges in absolute terms; they are much more likely to measure what they receive by comparison with what others receive. Hence, to bestow a reward on one worker is often to impose a punishment on his or her peers. Even casual praise may have this unintended effect.

The unintended effects of punishments are even more severe than the backlash of rewards. A punishment, if effective, undermines the position of the victim in his or her work group and thereby reduces that person's capacity for effective cooperation. It may also reduce the status of friends and peers, with remote and harmful repercussions.

The foregoing observations are not meant to suggest that rewards and punishments should be withheld, but only that they must always be administered with great caution. Praise and criticism ought usually to be private rather than public, and understated rather than overstated. Major rewards ought to be reserved for those whose right to them is universally recognized. Major punishments, as a general rule, should not be imposed on persons who are still potentially useful to the organization.

The foregoing warnings do not apply to rewards and punishments that are thoroughly routinized. By all means compliment the pastry chef on his chocolate éclairs *if* the quality of his work is such that you will surely be able to praise his deep-dish apple pie tomorrow and his brioches the day after.

5. *Give credit where credit is due.* This principle looks simple, but to apply it correctly you need a rather complicated formula for allotting credit and blame, which goes as follows:

Success should be credited to the entire work group, or divided between the entire group and one or several of its members. Failure should be blamed on the supervisor alone or on the manager and the entire group jointly.

The rationale for this formula is that the manager, having set out to elicit a collective effort from a group, should in fairness credit the group as a whole if that effort is successful. You may in addition acknowledge the special contributions of individuals, but you should not claim any credit yourself for the group's collective effort.

If the collective effort is not forthcoming, you must accept responsibility for having been unable to call it forth, since that was your primary task. You may or may not implicate the group as a whole in the failure, but you cannot blame individual members of the group without assigning them responsibility for the collective effort and abdicating your own responsibility.

6. *Listen to complaints sympathetically; never complain in turn.* A little reflection will show you that this follows automatically from the previous principle.

7. *Defend the faith.* The manager of an organization, as we have seen, is the custodian of its sacred symbols and the keeper of its moral character. This means that the supervisor must take the group and its work more seriously than anyone else and know how to assume a ceremonial stance for great occasions. You may be cynical and worldly-wise about anything else you please, provided you show an innocent and trusting faith in the value of the collective activity that you supervise. If you lack that faith, and cannot simulate it, you might as well give up and go into some other line of work.

8. *Develop an inner circle.* From the manager's standpoint, an inner circle of lieutenants provides additional eyes, ears, and hands to do his or her supervising. From the rank-and-file standpoint, the interposition of an intermediary who is partly a supervisor and partly a colleague makes it easier and safer to express complaints, suggestions, and requests. Traditional work groups almost always have an inner circle. But a circle ought to have at least three members. *"Tres faciunt collegium,"* said a maxim of Roman law; which may be roughly translated: it takes three to make an inner circle. If the group is too small to support an inner circle of three, the supervisor had better consider doing the job alone. A single lieutenant, or even two, may be more hindrance than help.

9. *Protect the status of subordinates.* Even a small work group without a formal hierarchy does not contain an undifferentiated rank-and-file. There are significant differences in seniority, technical qualifications, and authority within any group. Although it is not always immediately apparent, all of these statuses are part of the same structure from which the supervisor derives authority. So that unless you

respect the prerogatives of your subordinates and insist that others respect them also, you undermine yourself.

10. *Retain final control.* If, as a supervisor, you develop an inner circle of lieutenants and protect their prerogatives long enough, you may discover one day that you are no longer able to get anything done on your own. To avoid that, you need to retain an unshared right to approve (or veto) expenditures and personnel actions. You do not need to initiate them; you *do* need more than token control of them. Unless you have enough power to make independent decisions about financial and personnel matters, you do not have enough power for effective supervision. It may even be wise to act capriciously now and then in order to demonstrate your ability to do so.

11. *Innovate democratically.* Even the most traditional organizations require a surprisingly high rate of innovation to stay in touch with technological and environmental changes. In many cases, the introduction of innovations is the principal part of a supervisor's job, but innovation is hazardous. There are many ways of coming to grief while innovating, and some of the practices that otherwise contribute to effective supervision don't work here.

The effects of an innovation are always somewhat unpredictable. In default of omniscience, the supervisor needs to obtain as much information as possible from all the people who will be affected by the innovation and who have facts or insights about its possible consequences. Because any innovation in an organization affects some people adversely, or seems to, some resistance must be anticipated and the possibility of sabotage is never remote. Thus, every innovation, however trivial, needs as much support as can conveniently be mustered. As both field and laboratory experiments have shown, the way to muster support for an innovation is to bring all the people affected into the planning at an early stage and to give them a voice in the decisions that need to be made from the first to the last stages. Successful innovations are discussed, designed, and implemented in an atmosphere of participatory democracy. This may be difficult in an otherwise authoritarian organization, but it is always worth the trouble.

12. *Take infinite pains.* This is the most important principle of direct supervision, and the most essential to learn. Some people seem to come by it naturally; others acquire the habit by experience and practice. Inborn or learned, it is what distinguishes genius from mere competence and the great leader from a mediocre one.

The inimitable M. Pitard stationed himself at the waiters' counter and inspected each dish before it left the kitchen. Some dishes he sent back to the kitchen for more work. Similarly, Paul Strand, doing a documentary film about a Malay fishing village, postponed the completion of the final scene for a month because one fisherman got a haircut, and Strand was unwilling to go on with the scene until the fisherman's hair was the same length as it had been when the beginning of the scene was filmed.

The Contrast Between Direct and Indirect Supervision

Indirect supervision always involves the direct supervision of immediate subordinates, and, as we shall presently see, some of the same principles apply to both modes of supervision. The differences, however, are as important as the similarities. It happens often that people who have been promoted to high positions because of a talent for direct supervision fail miserably at indirect supervision. The reverse case is less commmon but not excessively rare. Some highly successful managers of great organizations have been inept as direct supervisors—for example, the first Henry Ford.

The most important feature of indirect supervision is limited power. The indirect supervisor does not have the means to shape the organization to his heart's desire, or even to understand it thoroughly. The basic patterns of work activity, the division of labor, the customs of the milieu, are constraints he cannot disregard and cannot easily change.

The medium and large organizations whose managers engage in indirect supervision are extremely diverse in structure and in patterns of authority. Moreover, the managers of organizations that look superficially alike differ greatly in power, depending upon their personal traits, the support they can muster in various constituencies, and the customary prerogatives of each position. But even the most fortunate indirect supervisor has only an imperfect and uneven control of the organization for which he is responsible. Many of its functions remain entirely beyond his reach, because they admit no interference or are not amenable to inspection or have independent bases of power. The president of a university, for example, cannot effectively supervise teaching and research in any academic department. At best, he or she exercises a slight long-term control over individual departments by budgetary means. In other large-scale organizations, such as manufacturing companies, fewer enclaves are protected by professional privilege, but departments have various efficacious ways of repelling what they regard as managerial interference. When challenges to indirect supervision become too obtrusive to overlook, they provoke a reorganization.

Reorganization often takes the form of decentralization, following a formula first devised by Alfred Sloan for General Motors in the early 1920s and later imitated by innumerable other corporations and noncommercial institutions.[3] After more than half a century, the Sloan formula still has an air of freshness and novelty and still represents an "advanced" management philosophy. The reason may be that the formula is genuinely paradoxical, giving much greater autonomy to subordinate managers with one hand while gripping them much more tightly with the other.

The general managers of the operating divisions of General Motors were in effect set up in business for themselves.

> The General Manager formulates all the policies for his particular unit, subject only to the executive control of the President. The responsibility of the head of each unit is absolute and he is looked upon to exercise his full initiative and ability in developing his particular operation to the fullest possible extent and to assume the full responsibility of success or failure.[4]

But this grant of independence had two important strings attached. Uniform accounting procedures were established for the entire company, and each operating unit was required to follow them without deviation, so that its financial situation was completely and continuously visible to the central office. (At a later time General Motors also imposed uniform personnel procedures and reserved certain spheres of activity, such as litigation and foreign marketing, for the central office. Later still, an overgrown top management began to intervene in the engineering and marketing decisions that were supposed to be reserved to the operating divisions—with disastrous results.[5])

Within the framework of uniform accounts, each operating unit was required to submit annual, seasonal, and monthly forecasts of purchases, production, inventory, and sales to the central office, where they were reviewed and occasionally revised. As the authority for routine operations was decentralized, the central office was vastly enlarged by the appointment of group vice-presidents and other executives exclusively engaged in "policymaking," and by the development of an elaborate structure of special-purpose committees to co-ordinate planning and operations.

The independence conferred upon operating divisions under this plan was not entirely illusory. In many respects they functioned as separate businesses, competing with each other, buying from and selling to each other at something like market prices, and developing their own network of commercial contacts with suppliers and dealers. But at the same time, the new financial controls enabled the central office to monitor operations very closely, and the enlarged size and weight of the central office enabled it to step in and reorganize an operating unit, or on occasion to abolish or merge operating units, without encountering much resistance. A similar formula—increased autonomy and self-determination on the one hand, uniform account-ing and tight monitoring of performance on the other—was eventu-ally extended to the shop floor in many large American companies by means of such devices as shop conferences, sensitivity training, and job enlargement programs.

The exercise of indirect supervision is obviously different in a py-ramidal organization of the military type or in a federal organization whose component units are more or less equal. The principles of in-direct supervision are more variable than the principles of direct su-pervision outlined a few pages back, and effective indirect supervi-sion is more dependent on time, place, and circumstances. What works well in one situation may be disastrous in another, as admirals discover when they try to run colleges and as industrial executives learn as cabinet secretaries. Nevertheless, there are some principles that do apply to all types of indirect supervision.

The Principles of Indirect Supervision

1. *Find and hold the purse strings.* Without fiscal control, an indirect supervisor is helpless.

2. *Develop detailed plans and projections.* The object is to measure the performance of every operating unit in a given time period against a prior projection, making sure that the comparison is clearly visible to all concerned.

3. *Develop personal relationships with subordinate managers.* This may be done either inside or outside the organizational setting. These relationships are desirable for human comfort, and essential in order to obtain information about matters not covered by measures of performance or output.

4. *Do your homework.* Compared to a direct supervisor, the indirect supervisor is necessarily deficient in firsthand knowledge of the operations for which he or she is responsible. This natural handicap should be compensated by a mastery of the wider information you can obtain by virtue of your position.

5. *Roam the streets.* Haroun Al-Raschid, you remember, was the caliph of Baghdad who roamed the streets of his capital in disguise to find out how well his government was functioning. In 1981, Charles Luce, the president of Consolidated Edison, pedaled around New York City on a three-speed bicycle wearing a meter reader's cap, to discover how things worked at the lower levels of that giant utility company. Such a disguise may or may not be practicable in a given case, but for effective indirect supervision you need to overcome your shyness and to look at the lower depths of your domain with your own eyes.

6. *Reorganize drastically or not at all.* It is nearly impossible for an indirect supervisor to transform an operating unit of a large organization from a position above and outside it. Units whose performance is unsatisfactory and cannot be improved by routine measures should be disbanded and replaced. The indirect supervisor usually finds it easier to carry through a drastic reorganization than to fiddle with minor reforms against the entrenched resistance of an uncooperative unit.

7. *Respect successful operations.* This is the corollary of the preceding principle. An operation that is exceptionally productive should be left alone if possible, even when some aspects of it appear unnecessary or crazy. When someone complained to President Lincoln that General Grant had been drunk throughout a successful engagement, Lincoln asked to know what brand of whiskey Grant favored so that he might send some to his other generals.

8. *Refrain from attempting the impossible.* No indirect supervisor is omnipotent; most are pitifully weak in relation to their organizational ambitions, and the larger and more powerful the organization, the less likely it is to respond obediently to its master's voice. The most important principle of indirect supervision is to concentrate on goals that lie within reach and to waste as little effort as possible on the worthier goals that are unattainable.

This last rule, baldly stated, seems ignoble and invites further explanation. The mythology of organizations includes a good deal of hyperbole and boasting. Unrealistic aspirations are often praised as if they were equivalent to real accomplishments, and this sort of rhetoric is useful in hopeless situations—for example, in the campaign of a political candidate who has no chance of winning an election. It helps the participants in such an exercise to carry out their responsibilities gracefully—and of course, miracles do occur so that a candidate ought never to be openly cynical about his or her prospects. But since, as an indirect supervisor, you have more to gain from organizational success than anyone else, and more to lose by organizational failure, it is generally better for you to promote collective aspirations that lie within the limits of the possible than to encourage hopes that are certain to be disappointed.

9. *Innovate boldly, but not often.* It follows from the foregoing discussion that the indirect supervisor has only a limited ability to jar an organization out of its groove of custom. To do so at all, you must make some changes, but from your standpoint, all changes are costly and time consuming. They arouse resistance and have unintended effects which you can seldom anticipate completely or even fully understand after they have occurred. On the other hand, since all innovations are potentially dangerous, there is no reason to make piddling ones.

The risk of innovating can be considerably mitigated by extensive consultation and by the development of as much consensus as possible before, during, and after the introduction of a new rule, a new piece of equipment, a new procedure, or a new policy. Consultation works much better when it is genuine; that is, when the advice of the consultees is heeded and the proposed innovation is modified accordingly. But even insincere consultation is much better than none at all. People whose advice has been sought are much more likely to accept an innovation than those who have no advance knowledge of it at all. Moreover, the development of channels for consultation seems to make the next innovation much easier, and may even, under very favorable conditions, lead to a happy pattern of engineering from below, or upward planning.

Let us turn now to some of the problems you may encounter as an indirect supervisor when you attempt to use your limited authority to maximize productivity.

Maximizing Productivity

The organization, as we keep saying, is not really a machine, because it is composed of living people, but it functions in some respects like a machine, because it is a set of interlocking parts designed for a particular purpose. Regarding it as a quasi-machine, the operator is led to ask a number of questions about its potential productivity, for example: What is the maximum output under existing conditions? or, How much could output be raised by the installation of new equipment or the installation of new procedures?

These same questions come up in connection with real machines and are moderately difficult to answer. They are much harder to answer for a quasi-machine, primarily because the human parts resist being operated at maximum capacity. This resistance is both obvious and subtle, individual and social, deliberate and unconscious. Overcoming it is the principal activity of the indirect supervisor, and you must use both obvious and subtle methods.

Estimating Potential Productivity

There are two rough but useful methods for arriving at an estimate of the potential output of an organization. The estimates obtained by these methods cannot allow for unforeseen improvements in existing procedures, but they do provide a starting point.

The first method is to break the work into its elementary components, time them, allow for necessary transitions and interruptions, and then add up those time allowances to determine the normal output in a standard interval of time. If it is known that a public-opinion interview takes between thirty minutes and an hour, that the average travel time between interviews is thirty minutes, that one hour a day is required to make interview appointments by telephone, and that the average waiting time is fifteen minutes per interview, then the maximum capacity of an interview team can reasonably be estimated at four completed interviews per interviewer per day. If it then appears that a given team averages only two interviews per interviewer per day, we may reasonably infer that its output could be improved.

The second method is to compare the average productivity of a working group with its own best performance or with the best performance of a similar group under comparable conditions. Either calculation may give startling results.

I was once asked to estimate the efficiency of a port battalion unloading ships by lighter in a foreign harbor under wartime conditions. The battalion had received a presidential citation for outstanding performance. Comparing the average daily tonnage of cargo moved by each lighter crew with its own best daily tonnage, we discovered that the battalion's average productivity ran about 12 percent of its maximum capacity. Further investigation disclosed every conceivable type of work avoidance, but the unit had looked efficient compared to other port battalions whose habits were even more outrageous.

It is not uncommon for a multinational corporation to install an exact duplicate of an existing factory in another country. When such plants are put into operation, some departments have very different output rates than their identically equipped prototypes in the original plant. In one instance, the metalworking department of a pump factory in the Netherlands unexpectedly turned out five times as much work as the prototype department back in Ohio.

Improving Actual Productivity

Nearly every productive organization shows conspicuous gaps between actual and potential output in some of its departments. Even after productivity has been systematically studied and improved, some large gaps will persist and new ones will appear. The improvement of productivity is not something that can be done once and for all; it requires constant effort.

In his book on *Raising Productivity*, Frederick W. Hornbruch, Jr. gives ten case histories of successful productivity improvement in industry. No two of them used exactly the same methods.[6]

The reasons that an organization, left to itself, tends to fall further and further below its potential productivity may be conveniently summed up under four headings: defective work methods, output restriction, systematic cheating, and snags in the work flow.

Defective Work Methods. The causes of defective work methods in apparently efficient industrial organizations were analyzed in the early 1900s by Frederick W. Taylor, the "father of scientific management." Here is one of his classic cases:

> The Bethlehem Steel Company had five blast furnaces, the product of which had been handled by a pig-iron gang for many years. This gang, at this time, consisted of about seventy-five men. They were good, average pig-iron handlers, were under an excellent foreman who himself had been a pig-iron handler, and the work was done, on the whole, about as fast and as cheaply as it was anywhere else at that time. . . .
> An inclined plank was placed against the side of a car, and each man picked up from his pile a pig of iron weighing about 92 pounds, walked up the inclined plank and dropped it on the end of the car.

We found that this gang were loading on the average about 12½ tons per man per day. We were surprised to find, after studying the matter, that a first-class pig-iron handler ought to handle between 47 and 48 long tons per day, instead of 12½ tons. This task seemed to us so very large that we were obliged to go over our work several times before we were absolutely sure that we were right. Once we were sure, however, that 47 tons was a proper day's work for a first-class pig-iron handler, the task which faced us as managers under the modern scientific plan was clearly before us. It was our duty to see that the 80,000 tons of pig-iron was loaded on to the cars at the rate of 47 tons per man per day, in place of 12½ tons, at which rate the work was then being done. And it was further our duty to see that this work was done without bringing on a strike among the men, without any quarrel with the men, and to see that the men were happier and better contented when loading at the new rate of 47 tons than they were when loading at the old rate of 12½ tons.[7]

Taylor's method was to observe the seventy-five men for several days, then pick out and investigate four of the strongest, finally selecting the one who seemed most interested in getting higher pay. This laborer, Schmidt, was then persuaded to work under very close supervision in return for a 60 percent increase in his daily wages. One of Taylor's men stood over him with a stopwatch all day long saying, "Now pick up the pig and walk, now sit down and rest, now walk, now rest," until Schmidt got the hang of it and began to average 47½ tons a day. One worker after another was picked out and trained to handle pig iron in the same way. The secret, as Taylor explained it, was that a man doing work this heavy had to be entirely free from load for more than half of his working time in order to avoid cumulative muscular fatigue. Previously, Schmidt and his fellows had worked themselves into a state of exhaustion early in the day by taking insufficient rest.

There seem to have been two other reasons for the improvement. First, by demonstrating the feasibility of a much higher work rate, Taylor changed the ideas of all concerned about what constituted a fair day's work. Second, in the course of his man-by-man training program, he eliminated those members of the original crew who were unwilling or unable to keep up with the new pace.

Stated more generally, Taylor's conclusions were that: (1) human capabilities in a particular kind of work must be determined experimentally—they are not intuitively obvious, either to workers or observers; (2) a worker cannot achieve his or her potential output in a given job without systematic training, based upon a prior study of the component steps of the job and the sequence in which they are performed; (3) to achieve high average productivity, workers must be carefully selected according to their fitness for a particular kind of work.

The industrial managers of Taylor's time reacted with enthusiasm to these suggestions. Time-and-motion studies, human engineering, and personnel testing flourished. By and large, these new methods were effective in raising productivity, although not quite as effective as their promoters anticipated. Even as Taylor wrote, the nature of industrial work and the composition of the American labor force were changing rapidly. Jobs as simple as Schmidt's were being taken over by conveyor belts and lift trucks. The winding down of immigration and the great increase in secondary education began to narrow the cultural gap between managers and workers. Within a very few years, Taylor's condescension toward Schmidt and his other subjects would sound hopelessly old-fashioned. "The workman who is best suited for handling pig iron," Taylor wrote, "is unable to understand the real science of doing this class of work. He is so stupid that the word 'percentage' has no meaning for him, and he must consequently be trained by a man more intelligent than himself."[8]

Some of Taylor's findings, however, are still valid today. It is still the case that in the absence of systematic job analysis and job training, the output of most workers and work groups does not come anywhere near their maximum capacity, even when they make a maximum effort. But as more was learned about industrial sociology, it became apparent that productivity was affected by other factors that Taylor and his followers had overlooked.

Output Restriction. The 1920s saw the rise of a new school of industrial experts who advocated the improvement of human relations in the factory as a basic method of improving productivity. Their principal spokesman was Elton Mayo, whose studies at the Hawthorne plant of the Western Electric Company from 1927 to 1932 led to a new managerial ideology, based on the belief that the productivity in any work situation is largely determined by patterns of social interaction among the workers.[9]

The experiments at Western Electric led Mayo and his collaborators to the following conclusions, among others:

1. The economic incentive is not the only motivating force to which workers respond, and not necessarily the most important.

2. Worker responses to managerial initiative are more often collective than individual.

3. The productivity of an individual worker is always affected by his or her emotions, which in turn are influenced by the emotions of his or her peers.

4. Peer groups form in work situations whenever the opportunity offers. They control production by modifying prescribed work procedures and by setting output quotas.

One of the Hawthorne experiments, the so-called bank-wiring observation room, illustrated in detail how the productivity of individual workers could be reduced and standardized by a peer group.

Fourteen men were taken out of their regular department and placed in a separate room to continue their regular work under close observation. Their task was to wire banks of terminals for telephone switchboards. Management set a standard output or "bogey" of 7,200 connections per worker per day and offered an elaborate scale of wage incentives to encourage output above the bogey. The operators, more concerned about stretching out the work and avoiding unequal treatment than about maximizing their paychecks, adopted an informal standard of 6,600 connections per worker per day. They arranged matters so that almost all of them were able to report an output close to this figure nearly every day, although to do so required continued adjustment of the pace of work, the transfer of work credit from fast to slow workers, the introduction of a play period in the afternoon, the corruption of the two inspectors assigned to the room, the hoarding of finished work for future contingencies, and considerable tinkering with the count of finished connections. Not all the workers participated in these arrangements, but most of them did. The net effect was that the fastest wiremen completed many fewer connections per day than they were capable of and reported fewer than they actually completed, while the slowest wiremen were given credit for more than they actually produced. Western Electric was, at the time, one of the most "scientifically" managed companies in the country, but the informal arrangements of the wiremen nullified most of the human engineering built into the bank-wiring job. Subsequent studies have detected output quotas enforced by peer-group pressure in hundreds of other factories and in nearly every other kind of large organization, schools and colleges, government bureaus and social agencies, hospitals and hotels—even in voluntary associations.

The restriction of output is such a natural response to organizational pressure that the people engaged in it are often unaware of what they are doing, and will deny the existence of an output quota when questioned. If the daily or weekly quota is set so low that even the least competent worker can achieve it without undue effort, it may take no more than a relaxed working pace and frequent coffee breaks to maintain a standardized, uniform level of productivity. If this does not suffice, the methods of the bank wiremen are likely to be called into play; workers who have finished the day's quota may avoid doing more work; work in excess of the quota may be transferred to less competent colleagues or hoarded for another day; breakdowns of machinery or communications can be neatly timed to fill up the unused parts of the work period; and so on. Which method will be favored depends on the nature of the job. For example, visiting nurses and appliance repairmen often develop masterful techniques of stretching out an early afternoon call until it is too late to begin a later call that might last beyond quitting time.

From a supervisor's standpoint, systems of output restriction are not entirely malign. It is sometimes advantageous to be able to count on every worker in a group for a fixed output of uniform quality. In a few occupations, like the building trades, the output quota has become entirely respectable; it is designated as a fair day's work and allows skilled craftsmen to work at predictable cost with very little direct supervision.

What makes output restriction a problem is not that work groups set informal quotas for their daily or weekly output, but that in many instances the quotas are scandalously low. Generally speaking, the more a peer group commands the loyalty of its members, the more uniform will be its work and the less variance among the members in output. Rensis Likert, summarizing the evidence from many separate studies in *New Patterns of Management,* showed that strong peer groups committed to the organization's goals are much more productive than weak peer groups in the same organizations.[10] But a strong peer group hostile to management or alienated from the organization's goals is likely to achieve spectacularly low productivity.

Systematic Cheating. The simple limitation of output by peer groups may develop over time into a complicated system of cheating the organization, involving several levels of authority and the active connivance of a large part of the work force. These practices range from relatively innocent rule evasions, like the hoarding of spare parts by shop foremen, to activities that are clearly criminal, like the pilfering of supplies for outside resale. In one teaching hospital that I studied, interns and nurses customarily borrowed small items from hospital stores and took them home. So many people were involved in this pilferage that it became accepted as nearly legitimate and was disregarded by the hospital's administrators even when they knew that, for example, ten thousand clinical thermometers disappeared every year.

The network of collusion required to protect a pattern of cheating may be extensive. In an industrial plant studied by Melville Dalton, shop supervisors were able to hoard spare parts and unauthorized equipment despite frequent surprise inspections ordered by higher management, because the inspectors, in order to maintain the goodwill of their local colleagues, telephoned in advance before each inspection and described the path the inspection tour would take through the plant.

> Notification that a count was under way provoked a flurry among executives to hide some of the parts. Motor and hand trucks with laborers and skilled workers who could be spared were assembled in a given department. Then, materials not to be counted were moved to: (1) little known and inaccessible spots in the plant; (2) basements and pits that were dirty and therefore unlikely to be examined; (3) departments that had already been inspected but could be approached circuitously while the counters were en route between the official storage areas; and (4) areas where other materials and supplies might be used as a camouflage for parts.[11]

Dalton comments that cooperation among shop supervisors to use each other's hiding places and to move workers and materials from one shop to another during these exercises was notably smoother than their cooperation in carrying out official duties.

A frightening example of systematic cheating that implicated an entire work force in a pattern of criminal activity comes from a study by Joseph Bensman and Israel Gerver of a factory producing wing assemblies for air force planes.[12] In that ill-starred establishment, new workers were systematically taught how to use a steel tool called a tap to cut new threads into lock nuts whenever the parts of a wing to be assembled did not line up well enough to be bolted together in the proper way. These tapped connections, of course, would be weaker than the specifications called for and in many cases would conceal a structural defect—unlike connections made in the proper way, they might loosen and come apart under vibration in flight.

The formal rules of the plant defined taps as criminal instruments. The mere possession of one made a worker subject to instant dismissal—in theory. In practice, as the investigators found, new workers were routinely shown how to use taps and how to conceal their use from plant inspectors, who were nevertheless fully aware that taps were in general use. Foremen not only winked at the practice, but often suggested that workers use a tap to complete a difficult assembly. On occasion they used taps themselves in the presence of workers rather than permit a partly completed assembly to be taken apart and started again. All taps, of course, were privately bought and smuggled into the plant by individual workers, but the official tool crib carried a large supply of tap extractors for the sole purpose of extracting taps when they jammed and broke.

A worker might be severely reprimanded for using a tap by the same foreman who had suggested that he do so, but the reprimand was understood by all concerned to be for his indiscretion in allowing himself to be observed. Actual dismissals for this cause were unknown.

The ultimate responsibility for enforcing the antitap rule did not lie with the plant inspectors, who were peers and close associates of the workers, but with the air force inspectors who had the right to reject defective assemblies. It happened, however, that there were only two air force inspectors for a work force of more than two thousand workers. Wherever they went in the plant, the news of their coming went ahead of them. Tapping was then temporarily suspended, and workers who were known to be careless about concealing their taps were sent out of the shop until the coast was clear.

There is no automatic way to prevent systematic cheating in a large organization, and as in the case just cited, it can go so far as to undermine the entire work process.[13]

The usual cause of such an extensive breakdown is a gap of some kind in the line of authority, so that the contaminated operations are effectively insulated from managerial observation or control. This may occur when top management is distant from a given work site and has no local representative with sufficient authority to resist informal pressure, as happened in the plant studied by Dalton, or when, as in the plane factory just described, the ultimate responsibility for enforcing a rule falls on outsiders who have no effective authority. It happens sometimes that social distance between top management and the lower echelons leads to a situation in which management cannot observe activities on the shop floor, while management's actions, viewed from the bottom of the organization, look senseless.

A *Washington Post* reporter who trailed two roof inspectors working for the District of Columbia government as they moved around in their van discovered that the ladders they used in their work never left the roof of their truck. Their days were filled with long coffee breaks, personal errands, visits to friends, and dawdling around tourist attractions. Their job was to inspect the roofs of government buildings and to call repairmen when needed, but the procedure of dispatching repairmen on the inspectors' reports had broken down at some earlier time so that their loafing on the job made no practical difference.[14]

It is much easier to prevent the development of systematic cheating in an organization than to cure it once it has developed. Illegitimate practices that have become customary are likely to be defended like legitimate rights. The secretary feels entitled to take paper and pencils home for her children's schoolwork. The intern regards free thermometers as a routine perquisite. The foreman cannot imagine operating his shop without an inventory of stolen parts.

Where the rot is far advanced, the system of cheating may be so closely intertwined with normal operations that nobody knows how to separate them. The overriding consideration, for the wing-assembly foremen, was that they could not meet their production schedules without permitting the widespread use of taps. The standards built into the production process were unwittingly based on that practice and made no allowance for the expenditure of time, labor, and materials that would have been required to complete each assembly according to the blueprint specifications. It takes a moral Hercules to clean that kind of Augean stable, but the thing can be done, and *is* done innumerable times in the course of human affairs.

Snags in the Work Flow. The work performed in any organization can be described as a flow of events through time and space. People, equipment, and materials join the work flow at predetermined points and leave it at predetermined points. Whenever an entry is delayed, misplaced, or aborted, the subsequent course of the work flow is disturbed to some extent. The extent of the disturbance varies from a trifling deflection to utter chaos.

It is obvious that an organization's work flow is composed of the work flows of all its component units. Each subsidiary work flow has its own predetermined sequence of events and requires the entry and departure of people, equipment, and materials at predetermined points. At the risk of tediousness, we had better note that each subsidiary work flow is composed in turn of the work flows of *its* components, and so on down to the individual worker who, of course, has a work flow of his or her own. Here, for example, are twelve steps in a classically simple assembly-line task—assembling part of a thermostat[15]:

1. Pick up housing assembly with your right hand and transfer it to your left. Turn it so the black-and-white cog is on the left-hand side facing you.

2. Turn large, exposed gear with index finger of left hand until dividing line between black-and-white on cog dial runs up and down with black on the left.

3. Pick up the wheel with your right hand while you hold big gear in place with your left.

4. Assemble time wheel to housing, face out, with 6 P.M. mark on time wheel aligned to mark on housing.

5. Pick up cam shaft screw with your right hand. While doing this, turn your left hand over so that the back of the housing faces you.

6. Insert cam shaft screw into cam shaft hole with right hand.

7. Place housing upside down in holding fixture with both hands.

8. Pick up two self-tapping screws, one in each hand.

9. Insert screws in two small holes in bearing plate.

10. With screwdriver in right hand, drive all three screws home.

11. Remove housing from fixture with your left hand while you dispose of screwdriver with your right.

12. Place completed assembly to your left with left hand, handy for the next worker to pick up, while you pick up another housing with your right hand.

This description does not give a specific time for each operation in the sequence, but the time element is implied by a standard, communicated to the worker, of how many gear trains per hour he or she ought to assemble.

In some other instances, where the timing of successive operations is less obvious, the entire work flow is controlled by a schedule that specifies the movements of people, equipment, and materials, moment by moment. Here, for example, is part of the banquet manager's schedule for a dinner in honor of a foreign dignitary at a New York hotel.

19:00 hrs.   Velvet rope barriers in position west entrance.

19:05 hrs.   Extra doorman reports for duty to west entrance; head porter, maroon uniform.

19:10 hrs.   4 security guards in position curbside to enforce no standing, no stopping.

19:10 hrs.   Upper-side luggage ramp cleared for TV cameramen; head porter to check cable fitting.

19:15 hrs.   Switchboard to open and hold telephone connection banquet office to west entrance service box and lobby box #3 until royal party clears elevator.

19:20 hrs.   Outer doors locked open unless rain.

19:25 hrs.   P.L. and J.R. arrive curbside.

19:28 hrs.   Operator hold tower elevator ground floor, doors closed.

19:30 hrs.   ETA royal limousine, west entrance, four in party. Contact Captain Nem (red uniform).

19:31 hrs.   Pause on steps for TV.

19:33 hrs.   P.L. and J.R. escort royal party through lobby, with security guards.

19:34 hrs.   Elevator away. P.L. accompany; J.R. notify tower and clear lobby arrangements.

This seems complicated for the simple business of getting four people out of a car, up a few steps, and down a short corridor to a waiting elevator, but it is perfectly normal for any event of a public character to be prescheduled to this extent in order to protect the participants against the effects of Murphy's famous law.

The snags that may develop in organizational work flows are too numerous to catalog. In the instance above, for example, the royal limousine arrived on time, but at the *north* entrance of the hotel, so that the TV cameramen did not get any pictures and the banquet manager did not catch up with the party until they had been on the tower floor for some time.

The problems created for an alert and well-tuned organization when plans go awry in this way seem desperate but are not very serious. The serious snags that appear in organizational work flows are more chronic, being ingrained in individual habits and group customs. They are difficult to remove. Among the common snags are useless work, unsynchronized fluctuations of workload, and irrational priorities.

Useless work occurs in every organization, but it is particularly characteristic of white-collar operations, especially those that have been running a long time. Its emblem is the sextuplicate invoice: copy one becomes the basis for charging, copy two accompanies the order, copy three serves as a notice to the recipient, copies four, five, and six are routed in various directions through various offices and eventually filed.

The connoisseur of red tape can easily find sequences of paper work in any large organization that require elaborate forms to be filled out, collated, collected, combined, and distributed without being read by anybody. These forms are eventually put in a file that nobody ever consults, without having contributed to the organization's purposes in any way. A variant form of useless paper work is the application of expensive cost-monitoring procedures to transactions too small to support them, as, for example, when the paper work required by a small maintenance job costs four or five times as much as the job itself.

Government agencies are particularly susceptible to this problem because of the pressure that is always associated with accounting for public funds, but it is commonplace in private companies, too. One large company that manufactures microprocessors discovered that when one of its engineers wanted a mechanical pencil that cost $2.79, processing the order required twelve pieces of paper and ninty-five administrative steps. This so alarmed the company, which was managerially as well as technologically sophisticated, that they shifted to a "stockless inventory" system. Instead of keeping a warehouse of stationery supplies, they set up an account with an outside stationer so that an engineer who needs a mechanical pencil now writes out a requisition and drops it in a basket for the stationer. The pencil is delivered the next day and the slightly higher cost is offset many times over by the savings in paper work.[16]

Red tape has more of a vegetable than a mechanical character, and its luxuriant growth can only be kept in check by periodic, drastic pruning.

Unsynchronized fluctuations of workload are particularly characteristic of production lines in which partly finished materials move from one department to another while undergoing a sequence of irreversible operations that must be performed in a set order.

Adjusting the rate of work in any given department to the rates of work up and down the line is, of course, a continuous problem. Whenever the work of one department is slowed by breakdowns, absences, or a shortage of some necessary item, departments down the line are forced to slow up and wait because they lack work, and departments up the line are tempted to slow down to prevent finished work from piling up. How often these slowdowns occur and how heavily they affect production depends in part on external conditions, like the seasonal availability of raw materials, and in part on the design of the line. A well-designed production line has a sufficient number of shunts and alternatives to absorb routine fluctuations in the output of its sections. Poorly designed production lines run at reduced capacity most of the time while their managers blame the weather or the union.

Some European factories like those of Saab, the Swedish automaker, have abandoned assembly lines altogether, in favor of a procedure called "group assembly" where groups of three or four workers spend about thirty minutes per engine doing a variety of tasks that they may divide among themselves as they please. But a group of Detroit assembly-line workers, who were sent to work in Saab's engine plant as an experiment, were uncomfortable with the Swedish method and did not think it would work in American plants.[17]

A poorly designed line may adapt as poorly to improvements of productivity as to work stoppages. William Whyte reports a sad little experiment in a toy factory, where a group of eight girls sat in a straight line spray-painting toys on moving hooks. They complained that the hooks moved by them too quickly, and to meet this complaint, the foreman reluctantly installed a speed control that enabled the girls to adjust the speed themselves. As so often happens in this kind of experiment, the average speed reached by these workers when they were allowed to set their own variable pace was considerably above the constant speed about which they had previously complained. But the story had an unhappy ending:

> Within three weeks the girls were operating 30 percent to 50 percent above what was expected for their training time, with the result that they were earning more than many skilled workers in the plant. The increased production of the paint room caused an excess of toys in the next process and a deficit of toys coming into the paint room. This caused so much dissension among the workers in other parts of the plant that the superintendent arbitrarily revoked the learning bonus and returned the hooks to the old time-studied, constant speed. Production dropped and within a short time, the foreman and all but two girls had quit.[18]

The design of production lines that can absorb normal fluctuations in the productivity of their component sections is accomplished by means of operations research, which may be conducted either formally—with heavy reliance on mathematical formulas and computer simulations—or informally—with pencil and paper and lots of arithmetic. In either case, the object of operations research is to achieve control and flexibility by counting and measuring all of the elements involved in the production process and getting a sure grip on the numerical relationships among them. The concept is applicable not only to assembly lines and other obvious examples of linear work flow; it can also be used to improve the meshing of parts in a school system, a newspaper, an airline, a library, or indeed in any large establishment where complex, repetitive work is undertaken.

Irrational priorities are characteristic of organizations of every type that have well-developed social structures and active networks of informal communication. In such organizations, rational priorities springing from the technical requirements of the work process are often overborne by the claims of status and the obligations of friendship.

The problem can be observed in the nearest convenient factory (or hospital, university, railroad, or boatyard) in which departments depend on centralized maintenance shops—electricians, carpenters, painters, steam fitters, machinists—to keep their equipment in good working order. All departments will claim as high a priority as they can for their own maintenance jobs. If department heads requesting maintenance work are allowed or compelled to distinguish between routine and urgent jobs, perhaps by a system of tags, nearly every job will carry an "urgent" tag, experience having shown that jobs tagged as "routine" never reach the head of the waiting line.

A closer study of the situation will almost invariably show that some departments receive consistently favorable treatment and that other departments are consistently discriminated against in getting maintenance work done, and that these outcomes cannot be explained by the relative urgency of their maintenance problems but can be explained by the informal status of the department head, his personal relationships with the maintenance foremen, and a variety of other factors that are more social than technical. To the extent that this occurs—and it seems always to occur—production suffers to some extent, since the jobs that are done first are not those that deserve priority.[19]

Problems of Quality Control

When a snag appears in a work process, the workers who cope with it often have a choice between allowing the volume of production to decline while maintaining the quality of the product or allowing the quality to deteriorate while keeping the volume of production up to the planned level. This is not always a clean, sharp choice, since varying degrees of compromise are possible, but it is a real choice that has to be made nearly every day in nearly every large organization. Many large organizations are heavily dependent on numerical measures of output to coordinate the flow of work among departments, and they try to hold department heads to their production quotas, regardless of circumstances. Measures of quality are much more elusive and indefinite than measures of quantity, and a deterioration of quality is generally harder to detect than a shortfall in the number of units produced or the number of services performed. Thus, there is a built-in tendency for product quality to deteriorate while production quotas are ostensibly met. When the decay of quality is sufficiently advanced, both managers and workers find themselves entangled in a sticky web of collusive and shoddy practices, as we saw in the case of the wing-assembly plant, which met its production quota by manufacturing unsafe airplane parts.

On a much larger scale, the sacrifice of quality to quantity has been one of the major obstacles to economic progress in the Soviet Union, where the whole unlimited power of the state pushes the factory and farm managers to meet their production quotas, while the central planning authority is too remote from the work site to exercise any vestige of effective quality control. Joseph Berliner relates an incident from the history of Soviet agriculture:

> For many years it had been the practice to take the livestock census on January 1. It would seem that January 1 is a rather harmless date; presumably it was selected by an innocent planner with the primary objective of facilitating schedules. However, the collective farms have targets of livestock holdings which they are required to meet, as well as targets of meat deliveries to the State. Ordinarily the peasants would bring their stock for slaughter in the early fall, when they are fattest from the summer grazing. But in order to meet their livestock targets on January 1, they kept their stock through the cold early winter months so that they could be counted in the census. The consequence was a disastrous loss of weight. . . .[20]

In a competitive economy, the consumer's tendency to boycott the manufacturer of a product when it turns out to be defective—and to tell his or her friends about it—exerts a moderately effective check on the quality of tangible goods, although it does not prevent careless workmanship or corner-cutting in the concealed parts of a mechanical appliance or the adulteration of food or chemical products that cannot easily be tested by the consumer. The tendency to sacrifice quality to quantity is especially marked in large-scale enterprises providing services to individuals—hospitals, telephone companies, social agencies, and schools, for example. The consumer has very little bargaining power vis-à-vis these enterprises and few ways of protesting effectively against substandard services, while top management finds it nearly impossible to conduct a continuous surveillance of operations from the consumer's perspective.

The only comfort to be found in a failure of quality control is that the workers who are at fault probably have uneasy consciences about it. When a manager sets out to remedy a deterioration in the quality of goods or services produced by an organization, he or she will find moral allies not only among those who suffer from the deterioration but also among those who are responsible for it.

There are three reliable methods of correcting a systematic failure of quality control in an organization. Sometimes they can be employed separately, but more often they need to be combined. The methods are (1) the revision of performance criteria to give more weight to measures of quality, (2) the systematic monitoring of consumer reactions to products and services, and (3) the enlistment of rank-and-file workers to plan and monitor a quality control system at the shop-floor level.

Most organizations are not very responsive to managerial rhetoric ("The primary aim of this Company is service to our Community, our Industry, and our Country"), but they are highly responsive to any criterion that is used to assess the performance of individuals and groups. If supervisors are rated according to their ability to fulfill a production quota, with bonuses and promotions going to those who overfulfill their quotas, and reprimands and warnings to those who fall short, most units will fulfill their quotas even if they have to destroy the usefulness of the product or service in order to do so. In Peter Blau's classic study of a public employment agency, employment interviewers were at one time rated by the number of interviews they completed, and during that era they interviewed a great many job applicants but found jobs for only a few of them. At another time they were rated according to the proportion of their interviews that resulted in job placements. Now they interviewed only a few applicants but found jobs for most of them. And so on through a series of changes in the criteria of performance, each change eliciting a reaction that was clearly rational from the standpoint of the interviewers, although not necessarily advantageous for their clients.[21]

Measures of quality are more susceptible to error than simple counts of items produced or services performed. But in the typical case, the difficulty is not overwhelming, and the extra cost of an elaborate system of quality control is one of the most profitable investments an organization can make.

Another method is to monitor the quality of products and services from the standpoint of consumers. Of the various types of social research useful in the management of organizations, consumer research is probably the easiest and the most informative. For example, pharmaceutical manufacturers' studies of the attitudes and practices of physicians with regard to particular ethical (prescription) drugs have invariably shown substantial discrepancies between the manufacturer's view of a product and the physician's. A drug conceived by the manufacturer as a substitute for morphine is prescribed by physicians as a substitute for aspirin. An anorectic (appetite-reducing) product designed by the manufacturer for the treatment of mildly overweight patients is found by a survey to be used exclusively in the treatment of extremely obese patients requiring weight reductions of a hundred pounds or so. A special iron-rich milk formula to feed anemic infants is unused for that purpose, but a small number of pediatricians prescribe it for all the normal infants under their care.

When physicians using any of these products are asked to specify the side effects that concern them in prescribing a given product, the list of side effects they give invariably differs from the manufacturer's list of expected side effects.

When the reactions of patients to the same products are surveyed in a similar fashion, their view of each product, their estimate of its clinical effectiveness, and their perception of its advantages and drawbacks are spectacularly different from those of either the manufacturer or the physician. The pain reliever previously mentioned is identified as a narcotic by many patients and they avoid taking it continuously for fear of becoming addicted. Patients disliked the anoretic drug because of its unpleasant aftertaste, of which the manufacturer and the prescribing physicians were scarcely aware. When it was prescribed, patients obediently bought it but took it only for a day or two, so that the effectiveness physicians reported in the treatment of extremely obese patients was illusory.

Even more fundamental than consumer research is the use of rank-and-file workers and lower-level supervisors as inspectors of their own work and monitors of product quality. As noted above, this practice is central to the Japanese system of industrial management and largely accounts for the competitive success of Japanese industrial products on the world market in recent years. In the United States and other countries where an adversary relationship between management and labor is part of the industrial culture—including, oddly enough, the Soviet Union and some other East European countries—the idea that responsibility for product quality ought to originate at the bottom of an organization and flow upward instead of being imposed from above is not yet widely accepted, but the weight of the evidence is overwhelming and does not rest merely on Japanese experience. It is simply not possible to maintain a satisfactory level of quality control unless the people who handle the products and perform the services have a moral commitment to product excellence and enough control of the work situation to get their jobs done right and enough sense of common purpose to resist the temptations to sabotage that will invariably be presented to them.

Choosing the Right Equipment

My friend Richter, the entomologist, lived for a long time in an Indian village in the upper Amazon jungle where the livelihood of the people was largely dependent on the canoes they built for fishing. The rainy season in that region is so humid that no man-made object escapes decay for very long. There are no caves or natural shelters in which to preserve objects, and there is no way of making permanent records. Nevertheless, an elaborate technique of canoe-building is transmitted from generation to generation. The way it is done, as Richter recorded it, is that every canoe is built cooperatively by six to eight men while a group of elders standing at the edge of the work site describe in chorus the traditional work sequence taking place under their eyes, and, on the other side of the clearing, a group of adolescent boys repeat everything they say. Meanwhile the workers silently match their actions to the customary words.

"Now the third boat-builder picks up the long adze," chant the elders.

"Now the third boat-builder has picked up the long adze," the boys repeat.

"Now the third boat-builder strikes the front end of the big log with a raking motion," sing the elders.

"The third boat-builder is striking the front end of the big log with a raking motion," the boys repeat, as the third boat-builder does so.

In such a traditional society, the selection of the right equipment for a particular purpose is no problem at all. There is only one technology available, and all the equipment is standard. The results that will be achieved when the traditional technology is carefully followed are known in advance.

Our technology is, of course, much more efficacious and versatile, but for that very reason the selection of the best equipment for given tasks is much more challenging.

The mention of technology suggests large-scale industry, but there are technological problems in every type of organization. To illustrate the point, let us take our examples from a church.

Nearly every church has bells in its steeple and an organ in its choir. These are durable items of equipment, but sooner or later the bells require major repair or replacement; and when they do, the modern congregation has an interesting range of alternatives—bells rung by hand ropes, bells mechanically struck, electronically controlled bells, or a carillon that rings convincingly without any bells at all. It is also possible to devise hybrid systems, such as one in which relatively small bells are rung by hand ropes but electronically amplified.

There is a similarly wide choice of organs. A few churches might still consider a new organ pumped by hand or foot, but the usual question is whether to buy a pneumatically operated model with a full-size set of pipes, or to install a small set of pipes with electronic amplification, or to go to a fully automated console that produces organ sounds without any pipes at all.

The decision is not easy. The cost of a carillon or an organ is very high in relation to the resources of the average congregation, and an error is almost irretrievable. Whoever makes the choice must balance the somewhat lower cost of the electronically operated instrument against the greater reliability and lesser service requirements of mechanically operated equipment. But this is not an easy calculation to make, since, on the one hand, the replacement of parts is generally simpler with an electronic instrument, but, on the other hand, the dependence on a particular supplier is much greater. The comparative frequency of breakdowns, which should be an important factor, is nearly impossible to discover in advance. The service life of a particular instrument, which might be the decisive factor, cannot even be estimated for the newer types of instrument.

Under these circumstances, even the most careful and judicious process of selection is likely to miscarry. The best rule of thumb is to choose the most durable equipment within the congregation's means.

The selection of a new carillon or organ also involves a standard sociological problem. It is obviously unwise to make those selections without the full participation of the bell ringer and the organist, but what is not so obvious is that the selection ought not to be determined solely by their preferences, since it is very likely that their preferences will not be pure professional judgments. Some preferences will be based on past experience—the organist who has struggled with badly designed amplifiers may be unwilling to consider the possibility that other amplifiers work well; some have to do with the conservation of status—the bell ringer who knows how to ring the old changes does not look kindly upon the keyboard carillon that makes his skill obsolete; some reflect ulterior motives—the organist reckons that the rewiring necessary for an electronic organ will let her install an electric heater under her bench. Whoever makes the choice must walk a fine line, taking account of the operator's knowledge and experience while disregarding the operator's prejudices. The situation calls for as much information as can reasonably be obtained and for a collective rather than an individual decision.

If it is any comfort to the committee of vestrymen, the same problem arises in much larger organizations—in selecting jet airliners, steam turbines, and nuclear generators, for example.

The proper equipment for a particular organizational task will generally be located somewhere between the crudest available equipment, which is clumsy, cheap, slow, and probably reliable, and the most sophisticated available equipment, which is expensive, difficult to install and maintain, and possibly not justified by the requirements of the work to be done.

The manager ultimately responsible for the selection of equipment must be prepared to resist two opposing kinds of pressure from the users of the equipment: on the one hand, a sort of Luddite resistance to the spinning machine that replaces the skillful fingers of the artisan; on the other hand—and much more prevalent nowadays—a craving for the fancy machine that takes no account of costs or benefits.

How to Recognize High Productivity

The yardsticks by which performance is measured vary according to the type of organization, but you can be reasonably satisfied about productivity in your organization if you observe that:

1. There is general agreement within the organization about how to measure productivity.

2. The measurements used are so sensitive that fluctuations in efficiency and effectiveness are detected almost immediately.

3. Most of the people you supervise directly do their work to your satisfaction.

4. Most of the groups you supervise indirectly turn out the volume and quality of work expected from them.

5. You often find it difficult to devise a reward commensurate with the outstanding performance of an individual or unit.

6. The reorganization of an effective unit is not likely to provoke resistance from other parts of the organization.

7. Operating reports are accurate and reliable. Systematic misreporting would not be tolerated anywhere in the organization.

8. When projections of future output are made, the actual output achieved is as likely to exceed the projection as to fall short.

9. An increase in output does not normally induce a deterioration of quality.

10. The organization is imitated by its competitors more than it imitates them.

11. Where output limitation is practiced within the organization, the limits are set fairly high.

12. There is no evidence of cheating, vandalism, or sabotage in the work process.

13. Rank-and-file members of the organization take quality control as seriously as you do.

14. Most breakdowns in the work flow are repaired without your intervention.

15. There is relatively little resistance to technological improvement if the persons concerned are consulted in advance.

CHAPTER FOUR

Morale

*You have lost your subject when you have lost
his inclination; you are to preside
over the minds, not the bodies of men.
The soul is the essence of a man;
and you cannot have the true man against his inclination.*
Sir Walter Raleigh to a Young Prince

Morale and Happiness

The morale of an organization should not be confused with the happiness of the individuals who belong to it. Morale is *satisfaction with an organization,* not with life in general. An organization has high morale when most of its members (1) accept its goals; (2) obey its important rules; and (3) choose to stay with it. Generally speaking, these conditions are favorable to the happiness of the participating individuals, but there are numerous exceptions.

High morale without happiness is characteristic of organizations that meet extreme challenges under strong leadership. The castaways of the *Bounty* mutiny, sailing their overcrowded open boat four thousand miles across an empty sea under the strict command of Captain Bligh, seem to have developed a very high level of morale, although they were not happy during their painful voyage.

Conversely, individuals who profit from the collapse of an organization's morale may be quite happy, like the Japanese corporal who, during the disintegration of the Japanese forces in New Britain during World War II, managed to enslave two officers and put them to work in his vegetable patch.

Under normal circumstances, belonging to a high-morale group is a pleasanter experience than belonging to a low-morale group engaged in the same activity, but it may not be as gratifying as alternative pleasures. The soldier who marches off to battle with his high-morale regiment might have been happier staying at home with his girl, but that is the kind of sacrifice that high morale makes people willing to make. Frank Smith reports a neat little study of which employees in the Chicago headquarters of a large merchandising company stayed home on the day of a blizzard. The job satisfaction of these employees had previously been measured, and it turned out, unsurprisingly, that there was a solid correlation between job satisfaction and willingness to struggle through the snow.

There is another important difference between morale and happiness. In most organizations, morale is correlated with rank, so that the higher the rank, the higher the morale, if only because the leaders of an organization have a larger stake in its program and identify more closely with it. But happiness is not subject to the same effect. It tends to be an inverse function of age, so that the junior members of an organization are generally happier than their seniors.

The most important distinction between morale and happiness, from your standpoint as manager, is that while you have no way of keeping all the people in your organization happy, you do have, or can acquire, the means to sustain their morale.

These means consist of ways of recruiting, training, and evaluating people; ways of rewarding and punishing them; and procedures for the peaceful settlement of conflicts.

Recruiting

Organizations, even of the same type, differ greatly in turnover rates and therefore in the amount of managerial time and effort that must be devoted to recruitment. Many American companies have a curious hybrid system, turnover being very high for blue-collar employees and very low for white-collar employees. In one large manufacturing company I studied some years ago, the median seniority was seven months for plant workers, six years for office workers, and fourteen years for executives. In a Dutch plant in the same industry at the same time, the median seniority was sixteen years for male employees at *all* levels but only three years for female employees, who customarily left the company when they married.

Other types of organizations show similar variability. The famous Bach Choir at Bethlehem, where some singers remain continuously on the roster for half a century, has an annual turnover around 10 percent, while other well-known choirs replace nearly half of their members from one season to the next.

Whenever turnover is high, the manager of an organization will spend a lot of time recruiting and the success or failure of his or her administration will be measured by recruitment results. When turnover is low, recruitment will take less effort but will be especially important for morale, since long-service members will be sensitive to any trends they can read out of the characteristics of the few people recruited—such as, for example, a decline in the choir's drawing power or a threatened shift from amateur to professional singers.

There is a tendency to underestimate the turnover rate in any organization that has variable turnover, so that participants are surprised by the rapidity of change in the human landscape around them. The manager who becomes closely concerned with the recruiting process may be able to mold an organization to a new image by the cumulative effect of routine personnel decisions more quickly than by direct reorganization.

Even when no such result is desired, recruitment offers extraordinary opportunities to the manager who wants to improve an organization. Most organizations do not select their new members in a wholly rational way, yet this is one of the sectors of organizational activity most amenable to a rational approach. The objectives of a rational recruitment policy are, first, to attract as many well-qualified recruits as one needs; second, to raise the value of the organization's human assets; third, to minimize the costs imposed when unsuitable people are recruited or when recruitment has adverse effects on the morale of people already in place.

There is little superficial resemblance between the curbside hiring of a casual laborer to help unload a truck and the worldwide search for a distinguished conductor to take charge of a major symphony orchestra. Nevertheless, certain broad principles cover both cases.

Let us consider how a manager who has an important position to fill ought to go about it. We assume that a decision has already been made to seek a candidate outside the organization, either because no insider is suitably qualified or for some other good reason. No wheel should turn in the recruiting process before that decision is made. To place insiders in competition with outsiders for a position is always a mistake and often turns into a catastrophe. It almost automatically undermines the loyalty of the inside candidates, even if one of them is ultimately appointed over the outside competition. By contrast, a decision to recruit from outside may be resented when there are qualified inside candidates, but it is unlikely to have serious repercussions unless an inside candidate has been promised, or thinks he or she has been promised, the position. Where there are several qualified insiders, each of them will normally regard the appointment of an outsider as a lesser evil than losing the contest to a colleague.

The best procedure for recruiting an outsider is straightforward, although moderately difficult to follow in real life.

1. *Determine in advance what qualifications are essential.* The unspoken corollary to this rule is to exclude and ignore all nonessential qualifications.

Let us suppose that as the director of an art museum you are looking for a new secretary and a new curator of sculpture. The essential qualifications for the secretarial position are a high order of typing skill and competence in general office work. These qualifications can be established by tests, references, and an interview; no special clairvoyance is required to make a rational choice provided you are willing to exclude such nonessential qualifications as age, beauty, race, ethnicity, class origin, formal education, and familiarity with the art world. To the extent that you take these factors into account, after determining them to be nonessential, you unreasonably restrict the pool of applicants and diminish your chance of making a good selection. The best candidate may be a young woman with a degree in English literature or a middle-aged dropout from a hospital office.

The essential qualifications for the curator of sculpture are, let us say, a wide knowledge of art history and previous successful experience as a gallery manager. It does not matter much whether the gallery experience involved sculpture, and it should not matter at all whether a candidate is divorced or married; male or female; white, black, red, or yellow; Protestant, Catholic, Jew, or Christian Scientist; chaste or lecherous; athletic or puny. Appearance doesn't matter, and so far as is humanly possible, you should pay no attention to the personal attractiveness of candidates.

Should age be taken into account? That depends upon whether you want a candidate who will hold the position indefinitely or one who will use it as a springboard for promotion. In the first case, forty might be a reasonable minimum age; in the second, forty might be a reasonable maximum.

Since the position involves the custody of valuable property and occasional opportunities for large-scale fraud, an absolutely clean record of honesty and trust ought to be required. But beware of unsupported inferences; there is no reason to assume that a homosexual or a habitual traffic offender is inclined to dishonesty.

To focus on essential qualifications and ignore the candidate's other traits calls for a surprising amount of moral fiber. Particularly when a position is highly sought after, it is hard not to be ruled by the spurious claims of attractiveness, ethnicity, and compatibility, and the practice of this rule is further hampered by the fact that for some positions, attractiveness, ethnicity, and compatibility *are* essential qualifications.

2. *Consider as few candidates as possible.* Every offer of a position, paid or unpaid, professional or volunteer, important or insignificant, tests a tiny sector of the labor market. If the offer turns up no applicants at all, this signifies either that the requirements have been set too high or the rewards of the position have been set too low—which are alternate ways of saying the same thing. In that event, it is necessary to enlarge the selection by advertising or other means, and if that doesn't work, to improve the offer. By contrast, the appearance of a host of applicants in response to an offer suggests that the qualifications for the position have been set too low or the rewards too high. The best resolution of this awkward situation is to raise the qualifications informally so that nearly all applicants are screened out and only a few remain to be considered.

The availability of a large number of qualified applicants may tempt the recruiter into a search for the "best possible candidate." This is always and necessarily a wild-goose chase; people are not really comparable to that extent, and potential behavior is never predictable with so much accuracy. Any serious effort to locate the best possible candidate is likely to turn up an overqualified candidate instead, someone too good for the position who will not occupy it very long.

There are several reasons why it is better to consider a few candidates rather than many, and preferably, one at a time, making a final decision on each before moving on to the next. The whole aim of a rational recruitment process is to get each candidate into sharp focus so that the people making the appointment can visualize accurately how the candidate would fit into the position. This sort of visualization is much easier with one candidate, whose history and character can be considered at leisure, than with two or three, and quite impossible with a larger number.

Comparing candidates with each other rather than with the position to be filled induces all sorts of distortions into the recruiter's perspective and, when collective judgments are made, any existing factions in the organization are sure to seize upon this ready-made opportunity for a fight. Considering one candidate at a time works much better. If several qualified candidates are available, they should be placed in rank order of apparent desirability by any reasonable method and then considered in order, each name being definitely rejected before the next on the list is taken up. If the people involved in the selection are unwilling to deprive themselves of the excitement of a contest—as they often are—the next best thing is to consider two or three names at a time. With more than that number, the selection process becomes chaotic and its outcome will probably be determined by accident.

3. *Make sure that the candidate understands the position.* It is by violation of this rule that recruitment most often goes wrong. Both large and small organizations frequently misinform the people they recruit as to the duties, privileges, and opportunities attached to their prospective positions. Out of eagerness and overenthusiasm, they may tell a few little lies. Of all the world's little white lies, those told to a candidate during the recruitment process are the least likely to be forgotten. They provide the foundation for a whole structure of future grievances.

In order to describe a position to a candidate you must make sure that (1) you understand the position yourself, and (2) other people share your understanding of it. If you try to do this carefully and systematically at the beginning of the recruitment process, you may discover that there is more ambiguity than you supposed in the position and that the personal characteristics of the last incumbent are perhaps deluding everyone into expecting too much, or too little, of the next incumbent. The resolution of these ambiguities to the point where the obligations and rewards of each position can be clearly explained to a candidate will do more to simplify recruitment than anything else.

4. *Study the candidate.* Years ago Reece McGee and I made an intensive study of how major universities selected new professors from among outside candidates. One of the findings of the study was that a faculty candidate's publications were the most important part of his or her record. But almost invariably, the people involved in the recruitment process omitted to read the candidate's books and papers in the course of evaluation. With a kind of sociable laziness, they traded unfounded impressions with colleagues who had also failed to

look at the evidence, instead of buckling down to long hours of tedious reading.

Considering any outside candidate for an organizational position, we have recourse to five basic kinds of information:

1. Biographical facts—generally presented by the applicant during the interview or in a written application, occasionally provided by third parties.

2. Official records—documentary evidence of the candidate's identity, birth, religion, mental status, schooling, citizenship, and professional certification, among other things.

3. Aptitudes and abilities—as demonstrated by many kinds of tests and evaluations, some obviously valid, like a test of typing speed; some rather doubtful, like an inventory of personality traits.

4. References—testimonials about the candidate's competence and character by trustworthy persons who know him or her better than we do.

5. The candidate's attitude toward the prospective position—generally deduced from behavior during an interview.

The organization rather than the candidate usually decides what specific information is to be presented in each of these categories. Every field and every organization has arbitrary customs of its own. Applicants to law school are often required to present character references from ministers and respectable neighbors; applicants to a graduate school of arts and sciences are required to present references from former teachers but from no one else. Candidates for the British Foreign Service were formerly required to take an advanced test in literature, including the composition of original Greek verse. American corporations sometimes ask an executive candidate to submit to a series of personality tests intended to reveal the profile of his or her subconscious mind. Some organizations select candidates largely on the basis of their responses to a critical question or incident. One firm of British merchant bankers asked every candidate, in the course of an otherwise innocuous interview, the following critical question: "If you were today given, or inherited, an income which would be completely adequate to permit you to live exactly in the way you wanted, and to do just what you wanted, what would you do?"[2]

The only acceptable answer was something like, "I would bring the money into merchant banking and make more."

Admiral Hyman Rickover, who for many years personally interviewed every young officer who applied to serve on a U.S. nuclear submarine, seems to have devised a critical question for each candidate. The story is told that at one interview he asked the candidate whether he would be willing to break his engagement in order to have a career in the nuclear service and when the question was answered affirmatively, requested that the candidate telephone his fiancée then and there to tell her the wedding was off. As soon as the telephone call was over, the admiral informed the unfortunate young man that the submarine service could not accept anybody who was so easily pushed around.

Even when a critical question is used to make the final decision, there is a great deal of preliminary information about the candidate and his or her qualifications to be sifted through first, and this is where most organizations, in my observation, do a sloppy and careless job. References, as every schoolboy knows, need to be verified. Few people bother. A telephone conversation is infinitely more informative than a letter of reference, but few people trouble to pick up the phone, even when important positions are involved, and few of those who do have prepared the questions they want to ask. To the professors who don't read the candidate's books, we must add the shop managers who don't ask for a sample of the candidate's machine work; the architect's clients who don't bother to look at what the candidate has previously built; and the churches that don't send anyone to hear the prospective new minister preach. It is commonplace for organizations to require an applicant to fill out a long life-history form full of prying and inquisitive questions, but to neglect to verify the applicant's name and address.

5. *Don't shilly-shally.* Neither the organization engaged in recruitment nor the individuals caught up in the process have anything to gain by dragging things out, yet this happens often, usually because the procedure is defective in some of the ways we have been discussing. The attempt to consider a large number of candidates simultaneously may lead to an impasse in which no candidate appears acceptable. Failure to describe the position clearly often forces the organization and the candidate to haggle wearily back and forth until somebody's patience runs out. Inattention to the evidence is likely to produce a standoff between competing candidates.

Most of these awkward outcomes can be avoided if the manager responsible for the recruitment process resolves never to accept a doubtful candidate except in an emergency, and never to delay the appointment of a satisfactory candidate in the hope that a better one will come along. While the search may be protracted when a position is difficult to fill, the organization's dialogue with any one candidate ought to be relatively brief and decisive. Nothing whatever is gained by keeping an ultimately unsuccessful candidate on the string for a long time. Much can be lost by doing the same to an ultimately successful candidate who then enters the organization without enthusiasm and without any sense of being wanted or having been specifically chosen.

Training

The various things done by organizations to assure that candidates for positions turn into successful incumbents are generally lumped together under the name of training. The term is misleading because it suggests a process whereby the trainee gradually learns to do exactly what the trainer wants him to do, as in the training of circus animals. The training of organizational recruits is a very different kind of process, and its final outcome generally represents a compromise between the plans of the trainer and the preferences of the trainee, further modified by the accidents of the training period, which are usually sufficient to ensure that the careers of any given cohort of recruits do not follow the same pattern as those of earlier or later cohorts.[4] Nevertheless, training is the term in use and we will follow it respectfully even when it leads to peculiar forms of statement, as in a recent textbook of industrial psychology, which has a chapter on "Training in Self-Knowledge."

In order to become the successful incumbent of an organizational position, a recruit must acquire not only the specific skills the position calls for but also a new image of himself and of the organization, a new set of social relationships, and a new code of moral values. The recruit who comes from outside the organization has a great deal more to learn than the recruit transferred or promoted from within, but also has the advantage of starting with a clean slate, while the inside recruit is called upon to change his map of a familiar territory and to abandon old friends and familiar ideas. This is a painful process and it often ends in frustration or failure. The recruit from outside, of course, may have similar problems if he comes from another organization of the same type in which everything was done a little differently.

In the vast majority of organizations—large and small, public and private, commercial and voluntary—the importance of training is underestimated and training procedures are less than adequate, with the result that many promising recruits leave the organization soon after they join it and the usefulness of many others is permanently reduced by a clumsy initiation. Indeed, it is easy to find organizations or segments of organizations in which nobody has been properly trained. I know of an office building with a large staff of janitors, none of whom have ever learned the right way to mop a floor or sweep a staircase. A study of a pediatric clinic disclosed that all of its resident physicians made the same elementary mistakes in attempting to communicate with the mothers of the infants brought to them for treatment.[5] In university teaching, it is a scandal of long standing that the inexperienced new faculty member receives no training in the difficult art of classroom teaching; he or she is expected to acquire it by instinct, which often fails, or by trial and error, which is hard on the students.

The reasons so many organizations neglect training are understandable. The trainee must be supported while producing relatively little. The organization may not be able to suspend the normal operations associated with the trainee's position while it waits for the recruit to be properly trained. The cost of scanted training may be great, but, spread over a long period of time, it is inconspicuous. And to confuse the issue, there are always a few people who seem to do very well without training.

Because the importance of training is so commonly underestimated, the manager who wants to make a dramatic improvement in organizational effectiveness without challenging the status quo will find a training program a good way to start. With normal turnover, it may not be long before the alumni of this training program have changed the status quo beyond recognition.

Successful training, we said, involves the acquisition of new skills, new images of self and organization, a new set of social relationships, and a new code of moral values—which involve quite different kinds of learning. An adequate training program must rely on a variety of learning methods and a variety of agents within the organization, including fellow trainees.

There are always new skills to be learned in a new position, even when the recruit is highly skilled to begin with. The organization knows, or can discover, just how it wants the task performed, and recruits can learn to do it that way if the trainer gets to them soon enough and stays with them long enough, and if they are given the opportunity and time to practice the desired technique until it becomes a habit. Nine times out of ten it doesn't work out that way. Trainees are allowed to develop their own techniques by trial and error, or by imitating others, before the trainer gets to them, and will then defend their own methods to the death. Or the training begins in time but is superficial. Techniques are shown to the trainees without sufficient explanation or without opportunity for supervised practice, so that they eventually improvise techniques of their own which are imperfect copies of the desired technique and to which, again, they become firmly attached.

Training, in sum, must be very patient if it is to be successful. Haste undoes the whole effort.

With respect to the new image of his or her own role and of the whole organization, these must develop in the course of the trainee's own experience—they cannot be imprinted on the trainee's consciousness from outside or above. But if these subjective images are to mesh reasonably well with the images held by others, and with external reality, the organization must provide trainees with a huge volume of information, much more than they typically think they want, and very much more than they would pick up unaided.

There is a kind of optical illusion whereby everyone from the top to the bottom of an organization is deluded into thinking that his or her own picture of the organization shows it as it really is. Because of this illusion, it is difficult for a manager, or any other experienced member of an organization, to visualize it through the eyes of a newly joined recruit or vice versa. The opportunities for mutual misunderstanding are endless.

We discussed in the previous chapter some of the things that you, as manager, might do to fill in the blank spots and correct the errors in your own image of the organization. What concerns us here is how you can provide the new incumbent of a position with an adequate map of the surrounding territory.

In the second chapter, I mentioned the air force division in which officers were unfamiliar with the official mission of their own units, and were uncertain about who reported to them and whom they reported to. Many of the enlisted men did not recognize the name of the unit to which they were assigned, or their own job assignments, or the positions of persons from whom they received orders.

Similar states of misorientation can be found in civilian enterprises of all kinds and even in voluntary associations. I discovered recently, for example, that most of the members of the governing board of a mental-health association could not tell whether the association was an arm of the federal government, of the state government, or of no government at all, and that they did not agree about the association's primary function.

Organizations in this condition are of necessity ineffective, and their members almost invariably have low morale because of the difficulties they experience in carrying out duties and pursuing goals they do not understand.

Orientation to an organization is a long-term matter. It takes years to learn the ins and outs of an established organization and constant study to keep up with its shifts and changes. Just as recruits who have no opportunity to learn the correct technique for performing an organizational task are sure to develop improvised techniques of their own that they may later refuse to give up, so recruits who are not given a full, accurate picture of the organizational structure and their place in it will invent a distorted picture or acquire one from equally ignorant colleagues and then cling to it with astonishing tenacity. First impressions are as important and lasting in the relationship between an employee and an organization as they are in the encounter of two individuals.

Any manager responsible for bringing new people into an organization must see to it that, at the very beginning, they are given a full, detailed, and intelligible account of how the organization is put together—its structure and program, its long-term goals and operating philosophy, the interrelationship of its units, its history and its plans, and the fullest possible description of the part the recruit is expected to play in the organization's program.

Only part of this information will be absorbed. It needs to be repeated when the dust of the initial encounter between the recruit and the organization has cleared and he or she is beginning to make sense out of the surrounding landscape, and then should be repeated again and again. No one but the manager responsible for the whole organization is likely to understand the full importance of this orientation, least of all the recruit, to whom much of the information will appear remote and irrelevant, and who, at best, will absorb only a fraction of it. Nevertheless all new employees need it, and the organization needs for them to have it.

Socializing the Recruit

It takes time and effort to help trainees acquire new skills and new self-images, but this need not involve any sociological stress. Helping trainees to acquire a new set of acquaintances and a new code of moral values is a much more chancy assignment. There is always a possibility that these new acquaintances will be hostile to the organization and that they will teach the recruit the moral values of an underground opposition.

The classic—and worst—method of inducting a recruit into this new social world is for the trainer to introduce him or her to a number of peers and then go away. The recruit is likely to be hazed, in one way or another, and the trainer loses contact with the situation.

I said this is the worst method, but in a few traditional organizations it is made to work fairly well by harnessing its defects. In the Coast Guard Academy, studied by Dornbusch just after World War II,[6] the new cadet or "swab" was subject to two sets of rules: the regulations and the traditions. The traditions were enforced by peers or upperclassmen. Although they involved prescribed infractions of the regulations, the swab was clearly informed when he entered the academy that he would not suffer for the breaches of regulation he might have to commit in order to obey the traditions. For example, when a swab received demerits for carrying out the hazing orders given by an upperclassman, other upperclassmen contrived to excuse him from official infractions until his demerit account had been balanced. (Since Dornbusch's time, the elaborate games associated with the hazing system in the service academies have been curtailed.)

Even if such a system works in a few institutions, most organizations are well advised not to turn over their recruits to an autonomous peer group to be socialized. Trainees should remain in personal contact with all the superiors who directly affect them, all the people at their own level with whom they will deal in their routine activities, and, of course, with any direct subordinates. People differ greatly in their ability to remember names and faces, so that it is difficult to specify how much contact is necessary to familiarize a trainee with a given number of associates; but it should be much more than is provided by a superficial introduction. The trainee who is expected to recognize the fifty people to whom he or she has been introduced as readily as they recognize him or her is certain to make some mistakes before they eventually come into focus. Mnemonic devices, like a table of organization with pictures attached, can be very helpful, but occasions for introduction should be repeated as part of the training program, until familiarization has been accomplished. These same occasions—formal and informal—provide an opportunity for the trainee's organizational superiors to let the trainee know in expanding detail what they expect of and what they can do for him or her. This information cannot be conveyed all at once. It has to be communicated bit by bit as the trainee's comprehension of the organization evolves, but it *must* be deliberately communicated. Information acquired by osmosis is sure to be incomplete and inaccurate.

Whether the trainee adopts the code of moral values the organization would like him or her to have depends in part on how the training is conducted and in part on the moral condition of the organization. The best method of indoctrination is undoubtedly apprenticeship—that ancient system whereby a recruit is trained by an experienced member of the organization who serves as teacher, supervisor, and model. Apprenticeship has gone out of style in some occupations, but is still widely practiced wherever people who hold positions of high responsibility are able to select their own successors: in the upper reaches of the government and the professions, for example. The apprentice acquires the moral code the organization wants him or her to have, with all its nuances, by imitating the master. Peer-group resistance to the organization's values is minimized, since apprentices are typically more influenced by their masters than their peers.

In a more impersonal training program, the transmission of organizational values to trainees is relatively simple when those values command full agreement within the organization (or within that segment of the organization to which the trainee is exposed). It becomes much more complicated when there is disagreement.

Organizational values are best transmitted when they are acted out, and not merely announced, by the people responsible for training, or by the people who become role-models for recruits. The manager of an organization is a role-model ex officio and may have an astonishing ability to communicate organizational values to recruits in fleeting contacts with them. That is the age-old secret of successful generalship, and it is applied every day by charismatic leaders in other fields, whose commitment to their roles is so dramatic that they strike awe into the recruits who observe them in action.

Another form of dramatization is the exaggeration of one or two organizational values. Violations are then represented as wicked and dangerous—as violations of a taboo. I knew a crew coach who so impressed upon his oarsmen the seriousness of breaking training that those who had done so generally went to him, confessed, and received an expiatory punishment.

Even in the most humdrum organization, there is likely to be some value that can be exalted. A supermarket, for example, may put accuracy at the checkout counter above all other virtues. A police department, although slack in other respects, may be fanatical about polishing patrol cars. Such values are always good for morale even when they involve some sacrifice of efficiency or effectiveness.

Like other forms of drama, the successful inculcation of organizational values calls for a nice blend of truth and artifice. In order for a value to be reliably transmitted to recruits, it must be held with real conviction by the organization's leaders and visibly exemplified in their conduct, but that is not sufficient. It must also be presented in an atmosphere of solemnity and excitement, and with the right background music.

Every high-morale organization has rituals, although they are not always immediately recognizable to outsiders. (A cocktail party can be as ritualistic as a procession.) It is particularly important from the standpoint of morale that the completion of training be marked by a ceremony that celebrates the recruits' survival through the rigors of training, formalizes their acquisition of a new status, and reminds them of their commitment to the organization's prime values. That ritual is sometimes omitted or scanted because the completion of training seems a trivial achievement to people whose training is far behind them, but it is the manager's responsibility to see that this singular opportunity for the reinforcement of morale is not wasted.

Here, as a negative example, is the way new employees were introduced to their work in the large furniture store studied by Levenson:

> There is no orientation for new employees. Members of the sales force are given an introductory lecture on company policies and benefits by a member of the personnel department and then shown how to make out a sales slip. They are assigned to a department and turned loose. The department manager is supposed to assign one of the older employees to the newer member to show him around but this is seldom done. The person has to discover on his own where the toilets are, where the cafeteria is, and what time he may take his breaks. Sometimes the outcome is embarrassing. . . . A new employee in the stockroom is given a quick tour by the supervisor to obtain a general impression where the merchandise is located. Then he is on his own. From our observation of the stockroom set-

ting, many new stock people seem to wander for days through the maze of stock before someone takes them in hand and shows them where the merchandise is located.[7]

Evaluating Individual Performance

The evaluation of an individual's performance in an organization begins with initial training and continues to retirement—and sometimes beyond. Every organization has to evaluate performance all the time, but it is nearly impossible to do it accurately; evaluation always involves errors. Some of these errors destroy the happiness of individuals, while others undermine the organization. There is no way of avoiding errors of evaluation, but something can be done to minimize the damage they cause, as we shall presently see.

The simplest and least troublesome situation is that the new incumbent of a position turns out to lack the bare qualifications for his or her duties. A summer camp hires a bugler who says he is a little rusty but will recover his skill. After three or four days, his bugle calls are still slow and quavering. What you need is another bugler.

It sometimes happens that the new incumbent of an important position proves almost at once to be unqualified. I know a college president whose hopeless incompetence was obvious within a month of his inauguration. A half-serious popular book has been written to expound the proposition that people in hierarchies tend to be promoted beyond their levels of competence.[8] The fully incompetent incumbent of a major position may be difficult or impossible to dislodge, but the problem is not so much to evaluate the person's performance as to live with it. It is likely that that person arrived at such present eminence because of a mistaken evaluation of performance in the past, or a whole series of mistaken evaluations.

Mistakes in the evaluation of individual performance—not permissible differences of opinion but forthright errors—occur for a variety of reasons and are partly preventable. They come in two styles: favorable ratings of incompetent performance and unfavorable ratings of competent performance. But since they have similar causes, we may as well consider them together.

Causes of Mistaken Evaluations

1. The Illusion of Consistency. There is a natural tendency, which seems to be automatically reinforced within organizations, to expect more consistent behavior from other people than our experience with them would predict, and to perceive more consistency in their behavior than they actually display. Nearly every appraisal of an individual's performance in an organizational position is subject to the halo effect produced by this illusion. The individual who does one thing conspicuously well or badly is presumed, without evidence, to be meeting his or her other responsibilities the same way. The individual who was conscientious and hardworking last year is described without hesitation as being conscientious and hardworking this year, even when his or her conduct has drastically changed.

There is a mountain of evidence from social science research and from history to indicate that inconsistency is normal. Consider, for example, the proofreaders whose performance was studied by Lawshe and McGinley.[9] The printing company that employed them proposed three criteria to measure the performance of a proofreader: average output, rate of error, and versatility. Each of these measures was accurate and reliable, but there was no appreciable correlation among them. In other words, a fast proofreader was no more likely to be versatile than a slow proofreader; an accurate proofreader was as likely to be fast as slow, and so on.

Or consider Captain Bligh after he provoked the crew of the *Bounty* to mutiny. He led the sailors who were cast away with him in an open boat to safety in one of the most successful voyages in the annals of the sea. His inconsistency was habitual: the detailed accounts of that immortal boat voyage report that while Bligh inspired his crew at sea, he quarreled dangerously with them each time they stopped at an island. Bligh provoked two other mutinies in other places before he retired as a rear admiral, yet he inspired many subordinates to admiring devotion. How would you rate him as a leader?

The inconsistency of individual performance over time is so well established that it can be expressed as a kind of statistical law. There have been thousands of studies of the relationships between high school grades and college grades, between success in job training and success on the job, between conduct in prison and behavior on parole, between vote-getting ability and legislative productivity, as well as innumerable studies relating the achievements of individuals at one time to their achievements at some later time. All these studies show a correlation ceiling of approximately .60 between measures of past performance and measures of future performance. The ceiling is easy to approach with any sensible prediction device, but virtually impossible to exceed. Statistically speaking, a correlation of .60 leaves almost two-thirds of the variance in future performance unaccounted for.* An individual's past performance tells us something useful about future performance but does not come anywhere near to predicting it accurately.

2. *The Masking of Individual Performance by a Team.* An individual in an organization necessarily belongs to a team, often to several teams at once, and there may be no easy way of disentangling that person's contributions from those of teammates or of finding out what his or her performance would be in another team. In the previous chapter, we saw how a factory peer group operated a system of output restriction that held the output of the most competent workers far below the level of which they were capable and at the same time credited the least competent workers with more output than they actually produced. Even when individual output is unregulated, and when no peer group interposes itself between management and the worker, most workers are engaged in collective tasks in which it is difficult to separate out the effective contribution of an individual, or in which individual performance can be measured but is strongly affected by the performance of others.

The case of the concert singer and the accompanist has been frequently described in musical memoirs. The accompanist who plays the music exactly as it is written will spoil the singer's performance without making her own performance look very good. If she follows the singer as closely as possible, adapting to changes of tempo and missed notes, the performance will go better but the accompacompanist's own musicianship may appear deficient. The accompanist who has a grudge against the singer can destroy the latter's performance without any visible effort. Although the singer's performance is somewhat more dependent upon the accompanist than vice versa, the two of them are so closely entwined as to make it hazardous to appraise either one without taking the influence of the other into account.

In highly dramatized activities like politics and war, it may be impossible to separate the performance of a candidate from that of the campaign manager, or of a commander from that of the chief of staff, even under the conditions of high visibility in which they operate. As we move down the line into the obscurity of any organization's lower depths, the accurate assignment of credit and blame becomes pro-

*The approximate proportion of the variance in future performance that is accounted for by past performance can be estimated by squaring the coefficient of correlation. In this case $r^2 = (.60)^2 = .36$, roughly one-third of the variance.

gressively more difficult, and whether the lieutenant or the sergeant deserves the credit for building an effective platoon may be a question not answerable this side of heaven.

3. The Masking of Individual Performance by Intermediate Supervisors. When an intermediate supervisor is required to report to higher authority on the performance of subordinates—as happens in nearly all organizations—he does not necessarily react in a straightforward way. From a knowledge of the organization's habits, the supervisor may anticipate that by reporting an outstandingly good performance he may lose some of the credit, or risk losing the subordinate by promotion or transfer, or disrupt an effective team because of the jealousy aroused by the special recognition of one of its members. The supervisor's motives for not reporting an outstandingly bad performance may be equally compelling. At best, he invites the suspicion of trying to evade responsibility. At worst, he incurs blame for the poor supervision that made the poor performance possible.

Moreover, both favorable and unfavorable reports diminish the authority of the supervisor to some extent by taking rewards and punishments out of his hands and by giving the subordinate a reputation the supervisor may later be powerless to change. A very secure, high-ranking supervisor may not be troubled by these concerns, but the ordinary unit commander, foreman, school principal, or chapter president reports very little about individuals to higher headquarters unless forced to do so. Recognizing this, most large bureaucratic organizations have installed formal rating systems whereby supervisors at all levels are required to evaluate the performance of their subordinates at intervals in writing and to send the ratings upstairs. Which creates some new problems.

4. The Defects of Rating Systems. Hundreds of ingenious rating systems have been devised and put into effect in modern bureaucracies: those with or without a forced ranking of the persons rated, with or without consultation between the rater and the person rated, with or without the participation of the peers and subordinates of the person rated. Each of these alternatives has its characteristic pitfalls, and a systematic review of them may lead you to feel that the whole enterprise is haunted, which indeed it is.

When the rater is not required to compare the persons rated or to place them in a rank order, but is allowed to arrange them against an absolute standard—for example, as outstanding, excellent, good, fair, and poor—there will be an irresistible tendency for ratings to cluster at the high end of the scale, with the great majority of those rated receiving at least "excellent," and nobody except the rater's sworn enemies receiving "fair" or "poor." If the competitive pressure is very great, "outstanding" may become the normal grade. This occurs, for example, in contests for fellowships when professors rating the work of their students know that anything less than "outstanding" will disqualify the candidate in the first round.

The skewing of ratings toward the favorable end of the scale is not overcome by requiring that fifteen or twenty traits be rated separately. The experienced rater will throw in an occasional "good" to break the monotonous string of "outstandings," but the net effect is much the same. The only effective way to avoid skewing is to require the rater to put all the persons rated in rank order of excellence, or to impose a formula that limits the number of high ratings a rater may give. These methods take care of the skewing problem at the price of making the system both inaccurate and unjust, since the best member of the worst group is then rated higher than the average member of the best group, against all common sense. The overall result is to depress the ratings of all individuals in good groups, as well as to stimulate jealousy and bitterness among co-workers.

Some of this bitterness can be avoided if ratings of performance are kept secret from the persons rated, and this is still done in many organizations, although less frequently than formerly, being now illegal in public agencies under Freedom of Information acts, and hazardous for private enterprises because of possible complaints or lawsuits alleging discrimination against women or minorities. One defect of a secret rating system is that it gives the person rated no opportunity for self-improvement. Another defect is that it allows a supervisor to carry out a secret vendetta against an unknowing subordinate and to stab him or her down without fear of reprisal. I knew of a case in a famous research laboratory where a section director accomplished the dismissal of a promising young scientist by a series of strongly negative ratings in order, as it turned out later, to create a vacancy for the director's ambitious girl friend.

The practice now followed in most well-regulated bureaucracies is for the rater to sit down with the ratee and discuss the ratings. One or both of them may be required to certify in writing that the conversation actually took place. This prevents a secret vendetta but makes a candid appraisal difficult unless the rater is so powerful that he or she is in no way dependent on the ratee's goodwill, and unless the rater is allowed to use an absolute standard and is not compelled to rank the ratee against close associates. The Greek legend of the judgment of Paris ("The golden apple for the fairest") illustrates what happens in any organization when a ranking of persons against their close associates is combined with compulsory disclosure of the rankings. The judgment of Paris, you will remember, provoked the Trojan War.

Some organizations, challenged by these profundities, have worked out a schizoid rating system whereby raters, in effect, keep two sets of books. A rating against an absolute standard skewed in the usual way is discussed with each ratee and plans are laid for his or her improvement. Another rating that places all ratees in comparative rank order is secretly prepared at the same time and sent upstairs to be used as a guide for assignments and promotions. Such organizations are wicked and deserve what happens to them.

There is an inherent bias in supervisory rating systems in that supervisors are likely to give higher ratings to their more compliant subordinates, even in situations where submissiveness is not relevant to good performance. In his *Management and Machiavelli*, Antony Jay devoted two chapters to this problem. The gist of his argument was that potential leaders are likely to be arrogant and stubborn subordinates; they are often forced out of an organization that needs leaders because of their unwillingness to fit into a mold of docile conformity.

One way to avoid supervisory bias in a rating system is to invite additional ratings of performance from an individual's peers and subordinates in order to obtain a kind of holograph of performance that can be inspected from any angle. This is obviously a sound idea, but it does not always work in practice. In the first place, it is almost essential that ratings by peers be kept secret in order to preserve the solidarity of the peer group, and that ratings by subordinates be kept secret also, in order to protect the raters from reprisal. But if the ratings are kept secret, they are only available to supervisors, and since the whole point of the exercise is that the ratings of peers and subordinates often disagree with the ratings of supervisors, that procedure is self-defeating.

Is it futile, then, for an organization to attempt to evaluate the performance of its individual members? Not at all. What *is* futile is the attempt to paper over inadequate information about an individual's performance with a show of objectivity. Before we consider better ways of evaluating performance, let us examine the most usual situation in which a deficit of information about individual performance develops.

5. *Invisible Performances.* Any complex organizational program includes many activities not ordinarily visible from the top, and some activities not ordinarily visible to anybody except the people directly involved. The normal tendency of the normal manager is to assume that these invisible performances are going well unless there is some reason to think otherwise, and even in that case the manager, like the husband of an unfaithful wife, may be the last to know what everybody else knows: that the cashiers are stealing from the till, the watchmen sleeping on duty, the mechanics working on their own cars, and the purchasing agent taking bribes.

The very worst maxim for a manager to believe is that no news is good news. In an organization, no news about the performance of an individual or a unit is sometimes good news and sometimes very bad news. I once observed a remarkable incident in the headquarters of a large voluntary association when one of the paid staff left town, settled in a ski lodge in a distant state, and stayed there for several months without attracting the attention of his immediate supervisor, who noticed his absence from staff meetings but concluded that he was "out in the field" and did not investigate further.

To assume that things are going well in any given corner of the organization because you hear no complaints and are not called upon to take action is always imprudent and may occasionally be fatal. The discovery that you lack solid information about the performance of an activity for which you are ultimately responsible ought to set off a quiet investigation without delay.

The Common Sense of Evaluation

The problems sketched out above do not have a single elegant solution, but they can be overcome in a practically satisfactory way by any manager who is willing to take the necessary trouble and to recognize and respect the sociological framework of the situation in which A passes judgment on B on behalf of an organization.

At the risk of oversimplification, the common sense of evaluating individual performance may be summarized as follows:

1. *Treat any evaluation as a useful estimate with a considerable margin of error.* Evaluations of individual performance are necessar-

ily inconsistent and necessarily subjective, depending upon what aspect of the performance is being evaluated, and when, and by whom.

2. *Refrain from evaluating with insufficient information.* This is a simple and sensible rule, but it is often broken. It is a little embarrassing to admit that one has no idea what a subordinate does or how well he or she does it, but it is stupid to form opinions without evidence and shameful to act on such opinions.

3. *Hoard information about anyone you may have to evaluate.* This means all sorts of information: memos, correspondence, interview notes, work samples, comments by third parties, recommendations, complaints, achievement tests. Even the performance of the most anonymous clerk in a large office or of a machine operator in a mass-production plant can furnish the material for an extensive, detailed, and highly informative individual record, as demonstrated by the employee performance record devised by Flanigan and Burns, and illustrated in Figure 6.[10] Such a record of significant incidents is at the other extreme from the usual rating scale and provides an infinitely better basis for judgment.

Another advantage of the significant incident method of evaluation is that it gives us a picture of the person evaluated in relation to the evaluator, and thus makes us vividly aware that every evaluation is the outcome of a two-sided or multisided relationship, so that no person ever appears exactly the same in different relationships.

4. *Never evaluate people you do not know.* This may seem self-evident, but in the mumbo jumbo of bureaucratic personnel practices it is often forgotten. The important implication for you as a manager is that with respect to anyone in the organization whom you do not know, you must delegate the task of rating that person to a responsible subordinate whose recommendations you are prepared to accept. If this undermines your claim to omniscience, so much the better.

Rewards and Punishments

The people who participate in organizations are rewarded in pay, prestige, and privileges, by which rewards their morale is largely determined. Voluntary associations that do not offer pay must satisfy their members with larger increments of prestige, privilege, or self-esteem.

Systems of organizational reward are extraordinarily complex and diverse. But the manager's fundamental problem in distributing re-

Figure 6. A Detailed Employee Performance Record

Work Habits and Attitudes

9 Productivity

4	3	2	1	1 2/6 Did job on time	2 2/2 Kept on working	3	4
5							5
6							6

a. Failed to do assigned task; b. Took more time than necessary; c. Slowed down unnecessarily; d. Worked at uneven tempo; e. Interfered with production line progress; f. Stopped equipment unnecessarily.

A. Worked efficiently despite obstacles; B. Was outstanding in the performance of his job; C. Avoided an opportunity to slack off.

10 Dependability

4	3	2	1	1 2/10 Checked parts	2 2/11 Told foreman when job would be done.	3	4
5							5
6							6

a. Left work without leave; b. Was late for work; c. Stopped before quitting time; d. Took excessive relief; e. Failed to report for overtime work; f. Loafed at or between jobs; g. Did personal work as job; h. Neglected assigned task.

A. Did extra work during idle period; B. Anticipated and notified foreman that he would be out of work.

	1	2	3	4
4				
5				
6				

a. Refused criticism, advice; b. Opposed instructions; c. Ridiculed foreman; d. Objected to, avoided, refused job change; e. Neglected to change desk, equipment; f. Was careless with materials, equipment; g. Kept same dirty, unworkable; h. Violated safety procedure; i. Distracted co-worker from job; j. Objected to, disobeyed shop rules.

A. Displayed unusual cooperation; B. Accepted disliked job without complaint; C. Accepted job change without resistance; D. Performed careful checks; E. Careful work reduced scrap, equipment damage; F. Salvaged parts, equipment; G. Cleaned, checked equipment for repair; H. Reported unsafe condition.

9A. Produced job on time despite inter-ference on new construction going on.

9C. Did not stop machine during minor distraction.

10A. Checked parts while machine was being re-paired. Saved time.

10B. Notified foreman job would be completed in two hours.

11a. Refused to try new, better method.

11g. Work table too cluttered to do job.

139

wards is the same whether it is setting wages or handing out medals. That problem, in short, is how to offer sufficient incentives to keep up the morale of the organization's most valuable members without thereby lowering the morale of everybody else. It confronts every manager faced with a request for a salary raise or a recommendation for promotion. The problem is compounded in most organizations by the need to balance the claims of seniority against the claims of merit and the need for parity with other organizations in the same set.

Seniority and merit are never completely compatible. An organization that does not respect the claims of seniority can expect to have high turnover, which is bad for morale, but an organization that does not reward outstanding merit will lose its best people, which is bad for productivity and everything else.

In practice, most organizations of a given type lean one way or another. Railroads and government agencies reward seniority more than merit. Their morale tends to be moderately high and their productivity low. Athletic teams and advertising agencies reward merit without much regard to seniority. Their morale tends to fluctuate with competitive success. Some organizations follow a mixed policy. A naval officer is rewarded according to seniority in the early part of his career, and according to merit later on. That sequence is reversed for a university professor.

The only organizations that can be relatively sure of maintaining high morale are those that offer an essentially equal reward to all of their members, such as exclusive clubs and honorary societies. In all other organizations, the maintenance of a high level of morale is a delicate and uncertain task, since productivity is achieved to a large extent by unequal rewards, which dissatisfy some members. It is the manager's responsibility to keep that dissatisfaction from turning into active resentment.

The distribution of punishments is as critical for morale as the distribution of rewards, and equally delicate. Most modern organizations are diffident about punishment. Schools no longer flog, churches no longer excommunicate, workers are no longer fined for breaking factory rules. In some schools, nobody is ever kept back a grade, and in some minimum-security prisons, the only penalty for misconduct is to be transferred elsewhere. Nevertheless, every organization administers punishments in one way or another, and the subtle punishments of permissive organizations are sometimes sufficiently cruel. The school that prohibits any form of corporal punishment may encourage pupils to ostracize an uncooperative classmate. Where organizations formerly punished their recalcitrant members by direct deprivation, the modern organization relies mainly on relative deprivation. The individual is punished by not receiving a reward that others receive. Instead of having his pay lowered, the worker is excluded from an across-the-board raise. Instead of being demoted, the offender is passed over for a routine promotion, or his name is omitted from the list of those who receive a routine honor.

An unintended effect of the modern mode of punishment is that punishments are experienced where none are intended. In one instance I observed, the promotion of a woman accountant to the position of comptroller was experienced as a punishment by her female colleagues, who did not concede her superiority; by her male colleagues, who assumed they had a prior claim to promotion; by the old-timers in the office, who did not expect to get the job but felt that their experience had been devalued by the appointment of someone much less experienced; and most acutely by the comptroller's two secretaries, who experienced a complex loss of social and erotic status. Reactions of this kind are so common that, in some organizations, every promotion from within is a disaster.

It stands to reason that you cannot expect people to be happy when they are passed over in favor of a close associate or when someone with similar experience and qualifications enjoys privileges from which they are barred. But as we noted at the beginning of this chapter, happiness is not the exact equivalent of morale, and, by the same token, unhappiness is not automatically converted into low morale. The catalyst is the sentiment of justice or injustice. Relative deprivation, when it is perceived as deliberately unjust, provokes disaffection with the organization. When it is not so perceived, the unhappiness soon passes and the effect on morale is temporary.

For these reasons, the primary concern of a manager in the administration of rewards and punishments must be to do justice, or rather, as Machiavelli pointed out long ago, to appear to do justice. But this qualification is not as machiavellian as it seems. It reminds us that the manager's private conception of justice has no relevance to the morale of subordinates. What matters is *their* conception of justice.

Distributive Justice

The sociologists who specialize in the study of organizations have had some interesting debates about the nature of distributive justice. According to one theory, the members of an organization perceive their treatment as just when the ratio of their efforts to their rewards is the same as the ratio of efforts to rewards obtained by other people around them, the effort, or "investment" being measured not only by sweat but by seniority, skill, and responsibility.[11] According to the opposing theory, the members of an organization perceive their rewards as just when the rewards are in line with their rank in the organization and their rank in the organization is in line with their qualifications.[12]

This theoretical controversy is not easily resolved by empirical evidence, although some ingenious laboratory experiments have tried to resolve it. For our present purposes, the points on which the two theories agree are more important than those on which they differ. Both theories say that the people who participate in organizational programs evaluate the rewards and punishments they receive in relations to the efforts they put forth, the sacrifices they make, their organizational status, and the rewards and punishments received by other people with whom they compare themselves in various ways. The essence of injustice is to receive less reward or more punishment than one expects on the basis of these comparisons. The key word is *expects*. "They did not treat me fairly" can generally be translated as "My rewards were less (or my punishments greater) than I had reason to expect."

The sentiment of injustice springs spontaneously from any serious discrepancy between how the individual expects to be treated by the organization and how he or she is treated.[13] When there is general agreement about what the norms are, the cry of injustice arises whenever the norms seem not to have been followed in a particular case or not to have been uniformly applied. During an organizational crisis, of course, the norms themselves may come under challenge and the organization may be accused of injustice because it follows a given norm when, considering its goals or its values, it might have been expected to follow another.

The members of an organization may receive very unequal rewards or punishments for nearly identical actions without provoking anyone's sense of injustice, provided that the inequality results from normal policy and procedure and is fully predictable. Indeed, it is probably impossible to discover any organization, no matter how small and simple, that treats its members so evenhandedly that the reward or punishment elicited by a given action would be the same for every member. Most organizations have complex procedures—some explicit and some unconscious—for assuring appropriate inequality. These are never so simple as just to give larger rewards and smaller punishments to persons of higher status, although their net effect may tend in that direction. For example, in almost every organization, a public expression of hostility to the organization by a high-ranking member elicits more punishment than the same expression by a low-ranking member.[14] The legendary "Man Without a Country," who was court-martialed and sentenced to lifetime confinement in exile for saying (under peculiar conditions), "I wish that I may never see or hear of the United States again," was necessarily an officer; the same comment by a common sailor would have led at most to a reprimand. On the other hand, the use of organizational facilities for private purposes by low-ranking members of an organization is likely to be severely punished, while the same conduct by someone of high rank would go unrebuked.

The individual's expectations are so critical in determining whether that individual perceives his treatment by the organization as just or unjust that a discrepancy in the person's favor may be nearly as demoralizing as one against him. Laboratory experiments show that when subjects in experimental work groups are led to believe they have been assigned a piecework rate of pay much higher than they are entitled to, their output drops sharply, and some of them quit.

The ratio of treatment to expectation is so important in determining the individual's attitude toward an organization that it often blocks out the objective advantages or disadvantages of his or her situation. An interesting discovery made by Samuel Stouffer and his associates in their monumental study of the American army in World War II was that soldiers in units with frequent and easy promotions, such as air force squadrons, were consistently less satisfied with their promotion opportunities than equally qualified soldiers in units where promotions were rare and difficult, such as military police detachments.[15] The investigators' explanation, which seems to fit the facts, was that easy promotions in the air force encouraged airmen to develop expectations that raced ahead of their actual opportunities, while the difficulty of promotion in the military police discouraged everyone from expecting it.

Nancy Scott's fascinating study of clerical workers under two styles of supervision found that an experimental group of clerks who were given considerable autonomy and allowed to work without close supervision had lower morale than a control group of clerks doing similar work under very close supervision. Interviews with the clerks in the experimental group disclosed that after they were given increased autonomy and responsibility they thought themselves entitled to higher pay than the clerks in the control group. They were so disgruntled at not receiving it that their output eventually declined to a much lower level than that of the control group.

Deleterious effects on morale can be produced quite mechanically by procedures that foster rising expectations and then cut them off. In bureaucracies of the civil service type, skilled craftsmen, white-collar people, and technicians are customarily hired at the bottom of a salary range with provision for annual merit increases, until the top of the range is reached four or five years later. The cessation of the annual increase does not put a stop to the habit of anticipating an annual increase, with the result that many employees quit the organization within a year or two after reaching the top of their range. Similar effects may be observed among public schoolteachers and, with respect to intangible rewards, among social work volunteers. Indeed, any organization that encourages its rank-and-file participants, or some of them, to expect a continuously rising level of reward is certain to have severe morale problems sooner or later when arithmetical necessity calls a halt to further improvement.

In most organizations, high-ranking members have much more to hope for than rank-and-file members. Their opportunities for promotion, remuneration, and honors are more numerous and involve much larger increments. It follows, by the same paradox we pointed out in the case of the airmen and military policemen, that they have more opportunities for disappointment, and that their disappointments are more severe. To just miss becoming executive vice-president is a greater blow than to just miss promotion to assistant janitor foreman. Thus, in most organizations, really severe morale problems are more common in the upper reaches of the hierarchy even though morale is generally correlated with status.

The disaffection of a high-ranking member of an organization may have calamitous consequences, as when a Benedict Arnold trades with the enemy for a promotion he was denied by his own side, or a Fletcher Christian uses his authority as an officer to organize a mutiny.

Up to this point we have spoken of the treatment of individuals and of their reactions, but groups, of course, also develop collective expectations and have them frustrated; and the excitement aroused in a group by such an event is amplified by social interaction so that, in many instances, the impact on morale is entirely disproportionate to the provocation. There is the typical situation in which a well-organized group suffers some small deprivation relative to another group but persuades itself, in the ensuing excitement, that its entire stake in the organization is menaced, and overreacts accordingly. Once aroused to a sense of having been unjustly treated, a group is not as easy to pacify as an individual, and when it has been pacified, its more intransigent members will probably continue to nurse their grudges for the next occasion.

All this adds up to a powerful incentive for any manager to avoid disappointing subordinates in the distribution of rewards and punishments or, in other words, to deal justly with them in their eyes. The principles of organizational justice are as old as Hammurabi and fairly straightforward, but cannot always be followed in actual situations, inasmuch as it is not always possible to determine who will perceive himself as relatively deprived by a given action. I know of a candidate for public office who was gravely disaffected by the emphasis that the state organization of her party put on the campaign of a candidate in a neighboring district, even though she herself had participated in a decision to funnel more resources to the other candidate, who was running hard-pressed in a close race.

How to Deal Justly with Subordinates. 1. *Respect the equality of equals.* The most elementary violation of rough justice—as every schoolteacher, platoon sergeant, and precinct leader knows—is to give unequal treatment to persons or groups who are entitled to equal treatment in a given situation. The key words are *in a given situation.* In most organizations, hardly any pair of members can be found who are equal in every way, but it is difficult to find any pair of members who are not equal in some way. The children of a family, being unequal in age and sex, do not expect identical Christmas gifts from their parents, but they do expect gifts of approximately equal value. The platoon noncoms have first choice of the available weapons but no more than an equal share of the available rations. The elected official has more political influence than the precinct workers, but the same single vote at the polls.

A manager ought never to create gratuitous inequalities between persons or groups who have a reasonable expectation of being treated equally in a given situation. Every manager does this some of the time—either inadvertently, because of failure to perceive that the assignment of duties or the allocation of resources in a particular way will disturb an existing relationship of equality, or intentionally, because of favoring some people over their equals. In either case, the discrimination is always perceived as unjust and usually perceived as deliberate. The morale of the people who are disfavored invariably suffers, but the morale of those who are favored is not necessarily raised.

Providing equal treatment to equals often presents a logistical problem. What is to be done when there are not enough schoolbooks or rifles to go around, or when only one messenger can be sent on a mission of special opportunity? The best solutions to such problems are mechanical. Since no distribution of unequal treatment to parties who are entitled to equal treatment can be intrinsically just, you should prudently refuse to be responsible for such a distribution and insist that the allocation be made by chance, as in drawing lots, or by rotation, or in some arbitrary order—alphabetically, by serial number, or by seniority, for example.

These last rubrics, if repeatedly used, turn into legitimate forms of inequality. In some schools, pupils whose last names begin with A and B will sit in the front rows of classrooms throughout their school career, while pupils whose last names begin with Y and Z will never leave the back rows. In some egalitarian organizations, like certain religious orders, the entire treatment of an individual nun or brother—their places in chapel and refectory, the work they do, and the privileges they enjoy within the house and outside—are mechanically regulated by seniority. So, in a very different world, are the assignments, routes, and work schedules of train crews on American railroads.

2. *Respect legitimate inequality.* The equal treatment of persons or groups who are entitled to be treated unequally is resented—often with fury—by the disfavored parties; to that extent it resembles the discriminatory treatment of equals, but there is an important difference. Whereas the favored party in the uneven treatment of equals often agrees with the disfavored party that the policy of favoritism is unfair, the favored party in the equal treatment of unequals seldom, if ever, agrees that any injustice has been done. *The natural tendency of distributive justice is toward equality of treatment.* If the ship's officers get berths with soft mattresses and the crew are given hard canvas cots, the crew may not perceive any injustice at all. The unequal treatment is conventional and contradicts no expectations. If the ship is remodeled and everybody gets the same comfortable berth, the officers will probably grumble, but it is inconceivable for the crew to agree that injustice has been done.[16]

In most organizations most of the time there is some slack, so to speak, in the direction of equalization. The removal of some of the privileges of rank will not arouse very strong resistance on the part of those deprived, if their authority remains intact and the new arrangements do not interfere with their work. Municipal officials do not rebel when their chauffeured limousines are taken away. But there is a line between equalizing the treatment of unequals and reversing the direction of inequality that a manager must not overstep. Suppose that some of the ship's officers are asked to sleep in canvas cots after the crew has been given soft mattresses. Or suppose that no parking spaces are provided for the private cars of the municipal officials who have just been deprived of their limousines. They will feel themselves driven to a choice between resigning and rebelling, and they will prefer to rebel if it is feasible. Either way, they will be moved to instantaneous hatred of the authority responsible for the decision.

3. *Prevent status incongruence.* Status incongruence is a condition in which interacting persons or groups in contact are unequal to each other in opposing directions within the same organizational program: for example, when A supervises B, but B is better paid.

Status incongruence is deadly for morale. *Both* parties in such a relationship feel discriminated against, and, as a number of empirical studies have shown, they are likely to develop symptoms of emotional or bodily illness if the incongruence persists.

We do not have the space here to describe in detail the psychosocial mechanism that creates these effects, but its essential features are well known. Given two plausible but mutually exclusive characterizations of themselves, people normally tend to adopt the more favorable characterization and reject the other. But when an organization imposes incongruent statuses on its members, this choice becomes impossible for them. Their attempts to choose the more favorable characterization will be frustrated by the party or parties on the opposite end of the seesaw.

Incongruent status cannot be eliminated from an entire society. It is one of the standard causes of human misery. The distribution of skill is never congruent with the distribution of strength; the richest people are not the most intelligent; talent and virtue do not always go hand in hand, and when they do, they are not always rewarded. But within the limited jurisdiction of a single organization, most statuses can be kept congruent most of the time, and glaring cases of incongruence can be cured in one way or another.

Indeed, most of them can be prevented by fair personnel policies, such as never withholding the perquisites and privileges that go with a particular position and never promoting a subordinate to a position of authority over his or her former superior.

Status incongruence is always less likely to develop if the organization provides its members with truthful information about their own prospects and is prepared to bear the costs of meeting its commitments faithfully under changing conditions.

4. *Keep promises*. This two-word sentence has all sorts of interesting corollaries. If every promise is to be kept, it follows that few promises should be made, and that is a good thing in itself. To promise rewards and not to provide them is a fundamental and flagrant type of injustice, as strongly resented in a nursery school as in an executive suite. To promise punishment and then to withhold it is a good way of losing authority. The keeping of both sorts of promises is the first requisite of a just administration.

Most managers promise too much to too many people. Enthusiasm, fear, or an excess of optimism leads them to promise more than they can guarantee, for example, to make promises that would have to be fulfilled by their successors in office. I know an industrial executive with varied experience who says that he has never assumed a managerial position without being approached by subordinates to fulfill promises made by his predecessor.

It is fraudulent for a manager to promise more than he or she can deliver, and the problem is not relieved by putting the promise in contingent form—"if we have a profitable year," "assuming that the board approves." The promise will be remembered, while the contingency is forgotten or regarded as a formality.

Because promises are so important and memory so deceptive, the rare promises that are made by a manager should be in writing or, when that is not practicable, before reliable witnesses. Without these precautions, you will sooner or later have the experience of making some personal sacrifice in order to fulfill a promise to a subordinate and still be accused of bad faith.

By the same token, a promise should not be ambiguous. To make sure that it is not, its meaning must be discussed at some length with all the parties involved.

The performance of a promise should be equally meticulous. To deliver a greater reward or a lesser punishment than has been promised is seldom advantageous. A promise made on behalf of an organization to one of its members is a formal transaction between the organization and the member. The more literally the terms of exchange are followed, the more likely are both parties to be satisfied in the end. This principle extends beyond the narrow scope of managerial promises and can be applied to all other transactions between the organization and its members.

5. *Observe due process.* Due process is a term borrowed from the courtroom, where it covers such matters as the right of a person accused of a crime to know the evidence, to confront the accuser, to summon witnesses on his or her own behalf, to have legal counsel, to remain silent, to appeal an adverse decision, and many related forms of protection that aim to establish an artificial parity between the excessively powerful state and the accused citizen, so that justice may be done.

Courtroom procedures are not suitable in the relationships between managers and subordinates, but the essential requirements of justice are much the same everywhere, and the procedures that ensure fairness in well-governed organizations are analogous at many points to the formal requirements of due process. Let us state them as flatly as possible.

No accusation or claim against an individual in an organization should ever be acted upon without hearing the person's side of the story, allowing him to examine the evidence, and assisting the accused to obtain evidence on his own behalf.

Confrontation with an accuser is an uneasy business in a hierarchy, especially when the accuser is dependent upon the goodwill of the accused in one way or another and cannot be protected against reprisal. But there are obvious dangers, and a whiff of tyranny, in the practice of accepting anonymous accusations or complaints. On balance, I am inclined to think that the identity of an accuser must be revealed when his or her testimony is part of the evidence, but may be concealed from the accused if the accuser has done no more than call attention to existing evidence, and no question arises about the accuser's credibility.

We will probably want to go beyond courtroom procedure in one respect by destroying all record of an accusation or complaint that is judged, after investigation, to be malicious or mistaken.

The appearance of professional lawyers in an internal organizational matter is generally a signal that the procedures of the organization have broken down or are about to do so. But every person accused, or complained about, ought to be allowed to seek expert advice and to have a friend speak for or appear for him at a hearing. Due process includes an inherent right to counsel.

An organization must respect its own rules when dealing with an individual. Its representatives may not reward or punish, convict or exonerate without following a sequence of appropriate procedures: examining the evidence in a relevant way, obtaining and weighing the opinions of people who are entitled to be consulted, and applying its own rules without deceit. This means, among other things, that as manager you should not connive at, or wink at, any arbitrary actions by subordinates that you would not permit yourself.

An essential element in due process is that persons in authority must take precautions to prevent themselves from following their own biases. If you want to be just you must delegate the right of judgment to others whenever your impartiality is subject to question. Among other things, you cannot judge a complaint directed against yourself, you ought not hear a formal accusation against someone you like or someone you detest, and you should call in others to evaluate the performance of anyone with whom you are closely connected. Whenever possible, provide channels of appeal for individuals from your own decisions concerning them. Such measures are often regarded as threatening by unsophisticated managers, but in practice they are much more likely to strengthen than to weaken managerial authority, reversing bad decisions and reinforcing good ones.

A serious commitment to due process will save an organization from the worst of those morale-shattering incidents that grow out of the maltreatment or alleged maltreatment of an individual and develop into raging conflicts between that individual's supporters and his or her enemies. But due process, by itself, is no remedy for other types of factional conflict that are equally threatening to morale, to which we now turn our attention.

The Containment of Damaging Conflicts

Outbreaks of hostility can damage an organization by lowering its morale or its productivity, or both, and by driving people out of its program. Aside from the harm an uncontrolled conflict does to an organization, your inability as manager to control it may lead to your overthrow, either by angry contestants or by impatient bystanders.

Conflict, of course, is a basic social process; there is no conceivable way of removing all the conflict from an organization. Indeed, the existence of cooperation *within* groups implies some degree of conflict *between* groups, and ordinary social interaction is sustained by a mixture of friendly and hostile sentiments. Most of the conflicts that take place in an organization do not threaten its ongoing program and are not very painful to the people involved.

Some sociologists distinguish among *episodic conflicts,* which are intentionally staged according to rules accepted by all parties and give pleasure to participants and spectators; *continuous conflicts,* which are unplanned struggles between parties in a stable social system who have incompatible claims on that system; and *terminal conflicts,* in which the object of the parties is to destroy each other. Episodic conflicts present few problems for an organization. Continuous conflicts present many problems but cannot easily be prevented. The managerial goal is to prevent the development of terminal conflicts.

Terminal conflicts in organizations need not involve bloodshed, although they may arouse bloodthirsty sentiments. In a terminal conflict between individuals, the object of at least one of the parties is to remove the other from their common field of action or at least to render the other helpless. A terminal conflict between groups involves similar motives, with the additional possibility that one group may seek to annex the other.

Once ignited, a terminal conflict is always costly. At best, the normal pattern of cooperation is disrupted for a period of time; at worst, the organization sustains a massive loss of resources and may break up entirely. When a definitive victory is scored in a terminal conflict, the losing side is likely to desert the organization. When there is a stalemate, both parties may be forced out. The full effects may be felt only in the long run, but even in the short run, any terminal conflict in an organization is likely to induce a deterioration of morale that spreads far beyond the immediate protagonists.

If you attempt to settle one of these little wars after it has gotten well started you will find yourself caught in the curious trap that Herbert A. Shepard observed in the management laboratory at Ann Arbor, Michigan, when two face-to-face groups of about a dozen members were given the same problem to solve competitively and a judge was appointed to listen to both solutions and name a winner. "Individuals may be good losers, but groups almost never are," Shepard remarks. The judge received no credit or thanks from either side in these contests. The winning group invariably thought it had the better solution and therefore owed the judge no thanks for the favorable decision, while the losing group attributed the decision to the judge's bias or stupidity.[17]

The same fatal mechanism may work against you if you attempt to arbitrate a conflict between two strong subordinates, with the embellishment that *both* parties may find your decision unacceptable and turn their combined fury against you.

A manager with the wisdom of Solomon may occasionally be able to suggest a settlement that is fully acceptable to both of the parties locked in a death struggle, but the odds against it are overwhelming. It is infinitely easier to prevent conflicts from escalating into the terminal phase than to settle them after they have escalated. The better practice is to concentrate on nipping them in the bud, and when that fails, to work on isolating the trouble.

Four Types of Conflict and What to Do about Them

The scenarios of organizational conflict are many and varied, but every manager has to deal sooner or later with four stock situations: (1) a personal feud between two key members of the organization; (2) the alleged persecution of a subordinate by a superior; (3) the breakdown of cooperation between two related departments; (4) a schism between ideological factions.

Each of these stock situations has certain standard features that make it possible for us to talk about what a manager can do to prevent or contain such disturbances without limiting the discussion to particular cases.

The development of a *personal feud* between two key members of an organization is typically marked by an accumulation of mutual grievances: the interruption, at first, of sociable communication and, later, of all communication; a growing paranoia, as each of them discovers the actions of the other by hearsay and interprets them with suspicion; and the recruitment of friends and associates to join the hostilities. The disturbance of normal working relationships eventually extends far beyond the broken relationship between the principal parties, so that the manager who succeeds in remaining neutral may be distrusted and eventually hated by both sides.

The best strategy for resolving a personal feud between two key members of your organization is remarkably simple: *take one side or the other.*

This advice may seem surprising, but a little reflection will show good reasons for it. We are dealing, remember, with an emotional crisis, not a rational argument that can be resolved by discussion. Many feuds do begin with rational arguments, but as the emotional crisis develops, the original issues are left far behind. Some feuds are not based on organizational issues at all. The most bitter feud I have ever observed in an organization began when one vice-president had a weekend affair with another's married secretary.

Once kindled, a feud between persons of approximately equal organizational power is not likely to be extinguished. Assuming that both persons are valuable to the organization, the manager who intervenes has a double purpose: to prevent them from drawing in other people, and to keep them both in the organization, if possible.

By giving full support to one of the feudists, preferably the stronger, the manager furthers both these purposes. First, the conflict becomes much less inviting to bystanders because the reinforced party no longer needs help and the other party's cause is much less promising. Second, the danger that both people may quit in anger is effectively averted. The one supported by the manager has no motive to quit. The loser may walk out, of course, but is somewhat less likely to do so than if the feud had been allowed to run its full course. It may be easier for the loser to make peace in the face of overwhelming odds than it would have been in a more equal struggle.

The alleged *persecution of a subordinate by a superior* needs to be handled differently, since the problem it poses for the organization is quite different. Whereas a feud out of control may split the organization down the middle, a grievance out of control may spark off a rebellion that splits it horizontally. Moreover, in this situation the manager is not much concerned about losing people. The alleged persecutor will not experience much pressure to quit unless matters get completely out of hand, and whether the alleged victim goes or stays is relatively unimportant to the organization.

The manager who wants to intervene in an incident of this kind has very limited options. If you support the alleged persecutor, who already has a preponderance of power, you create the impression of being indifferent to justice. If you support the alleged victim, you break the bond of loyalty between yourself and your subordinate and run the risk of alienating other subordinates who feel threatened by the incident.

The best method of handling an alleged persecution was suggested in the second chapter in connection with grievance procedures: *delegate responsibility for investigating and settling the complaint to an impartial agent.*

This has several related advantages. It protects you from taking action on a biased view of the facts, which you are otherwise likely to do because your relationship to the higher-ranking party to the conflict is so much closer. It protects the complainant from reprisals by his or her superior, and it introduces a wholesome delay that interrupts the accumulation of tension. And most important, it demonstrates that the organization is committed to evenhanded justice, which, as noted before, is the real foundation of morale.

The *breakdown of cooperation between related departments* of an organization normally occurs in connection with a boundary dispute. If we examine the development of such a dispute in detail we almost always discover that one department is perceived by another to be encroaching upon its territory and that the refusal of routine cooperation is either a device for checking the encroachment or a protest against it.

Such situations have to be investigated carefully before any action can be taken. A boundary dispute can sometimes be settled out of hand either because it arose from a simple misunderstanding or because one of the parties is plainly in the wrong. More often, it will be found that both departments have a reasonable claim to the disputed territory, and in that case, it is unlikely that the quarrel can be settled by bringing the parties together and letting them talk it out.

About the only way to put a stop to a boundary dispute is to *reorganize the departments or the disputed territory so that the boundary is unmistakable.*

As a participant-observer in a New England factory some years ago, Orvis Collins noted that all the executives were Yankees and all the foremen were Irish. When a central janitor service was established under the auspices of the labor-management committee, a quarrel developed over the question of who should be in charge of the janitor service. The labor members of the committee, visualizing the post as janitor foreman, insisted on an Irish candidate. The management members, who regarded the position as an executive one, refused to accept the Irish nominee. The problem was resolved when top management ordered the position classified as "sanitation engineer" and then, as a matter of course, appointed a Yankee.[18]

Such a proceeding may seem high-handed, but it causes much less trouble than the attempt to mediate a boundary dispute impartially. Most boundary disputes occur in the first place because of managerial confusion or indecisiveness.

The most difficult kind of conflict to resolve in an organization is a *schism between ideological factions*. One faction in the church wants to retain the traditional liturgy; the opposing faction wants the liturgy modernized. One faction in a civic association wants a stay out of politics; the other faction believes that the association's goals can be achieved only by political action. One faction in the union preaches long-term cooperation with employers; the other faction wants to give them hell. And so on. Nearly every live organization contains such ideological divisions, but they turn into full-blown schisms only under certain conditions, to wit: one or more ambitious and devoted leaders in each faction; an outraged reaction to some particular incident that provokes the mobilization of one faction and countermobilization of the other; the imminence of a major decision that seems to involve a choice between the opposing ideologies.

If you are manager of an organization split by schism you cannot remain above the battle because you cannot seem to ignore any ideological issue taken so seriously by other members. But neither can you support either faction without jeopardizing your claim to be the leader of the whole organization. The only way out of this dilemma is to seek and find a genuine compromise between the two factions, based on a synthesis of their opposing positions. Any other policy risks the organization's future, if only because ideological disputes arouse passions all out of proportion to the practical interests involved. "The reason why controversies of this kind are so terribly bitter," said Dean Courtney Brown in the course of an argument about educational ideology, "is that the stakes are so *low*," and indeed, there is some reason to believe that the less the protagonists have at stake, the more bitter an ideological schism may become, since there is little pressure to reach a compromise when there are no practical interests to be protected.

The strategy for resolving a schism in an organization may be stated thus: *Bring the factions together, force them to work out a mutually acceptable compromise, and then throw all your weight behind the compromise.*

This procedure is not foolproof, but it is clearly the best to follow. (The fools most likely to cause trouble are the zealots of either faction.) It takes a great deal of time, work, and emotional wear and tear to find an acceptable compromise, and, in the course of protracted negotiations, the representatives of each faction are likely to lose touch with the people they represent, who have not undergone the instructive experience of being forced to descend from their fighting platforms and grapple with the issues. I once sat with an eighteen-member committee appointed to work out a compromise between two bitter factions in a large public institution, the one favoring continued growth and the other demanding a policy of stabilization. Most of the members of the committee, when originally appointed, were fanatical partisans of one side or the other, and the meetings, under the chairmanship of the institution's second-in-command, began in an atmosphere of deep mistrust. But after seven months of meeting two or three times a week, often far into the night, and after examining thousands of pages of evidence and hearing scores of witnesses, the committee found a detailed compromise that nearly wrote itself. Things did not go quite as smoothly when the committee members reported back to their respective factions; some of them were roughly treated. Each faction developed a minority of diehards who rejected the compromise and those associated with it. But in the long run, and with strong support from the institution's chief executive, the compromise proved irresistible.

How to Recognize High Morale

The indicators of a high level of morale vary somewhat from one type of organization to another and are occasionally deceptive, but as a manager you should be reasonably content if you observe that:

1. In your organizational rounds, you never encounter small clusters of people who scatter furtively at your approach.

2. Although lateness and absenteeism occur, they never seem to interfere with the organizational program.

3. The turnover rate is stable or declining. Few people leave voluntarily except for compelling personal reasons.

4. The people who are recruited to fill vacant positions generally seem to be better qualified than the people they replace.

5. Recruits are absorbed very quickly into the informal social network.

6. Everyone in the organization seems to know what his or her job is, and agreement about the organization's goals is taken for granted.

7. Decisions to hire, fire, promote, or demote are usually unanimous, or nearly so, among those consulted.

8. Dismissals and demotions are rare and do not require elaborate precautions.

9. Ratings are not taken very seriously, but those in a supervisory position know a great deal about the people who report to them and are willing to pass such information on to their superiors.

10. There is relatively little discussion of pay and privileges. The existing distribution is taken for granted most of the time.

11. Organizational ceremonies are always well attended.

12. You are seldom called upon by subordinates to help maintain their authority.

13. People who get involved in organizational conflicts are apologetic about it, not complacent, and do not stop greeting each other.

14. Your intervention in a conflict is usually welcomed by both sides.

CHAPTER FIVE

Change

*Suppose that a football reformer observed
the obvious fact that the object of the game
is to make touchdowns. This would lead
immediately to the important discovery
that if the two teams would only cooperate,
hundreds of touchdowns could be made in a game,
while only one or two of them
are made when each opposes the other.*

Thurman Arnold

Change and Innovation

No organization exists in a vacuum. Every organization must submit to the demands of its environment, and these demands vary as the environment changes. There have even been more or less serious attempts to apply Darwin's model of natural selection and the survival of the fittest to organizations.[1] Even the most passive organization is compelled to modify itself from time to time in response to irresistible changes in its environment. A well-known study of a civic association was published under the title, "The Reluctant Organization and the Aggressive Environment," and the title tells the whole story. The organization in question sought to do as little as possible, but other civic associations pushed and pulled it into one new activity after another.

Impulses toward change may also appear in an organization without any outside stimulus. Organizations, like individuals, engage in campaigns of self-improvement. Many large organizations have planning departments to provide a steady flow of innovations.

Planning does not protect an organization from unforeseen changes: in the first place, it cannot control the external environment, and in the second place, carefully planned changes in one part of an organization usually cause unexpected stresses in other parts.

The most elementary forms of organizational change are growth and decline. Few human organizations come to rest at the exact equilibrium point between growth and expansion.[2] Most of them, at any given time, are either expanding or contracting. Within limits, both processes are cumulative. Growth facilitates further growth; decline paves the way for further decline. Turning points are relatively infrequent. An organization may grow continuously from the time it is founded until it reaches a turning point and then decline continuously until it disappears.

Growth and decline call for numerous adjustments in an organization, and that is where we begin our discussion of the manager's responsibility for adapting to change. Then, we will consider the types of adaptation required by market pressures, social change, technological change, and creative innovation.

Growing, Stable, and Declining Organizations

In some fields of activity, like banking and politics, an organization's growth rate is a direct measure of its success. In any field, the growing organization has certain natural advantages. Its expanding resources pay for past mistakes and offer protection against current risks. The enlargement of its program creates new opportunities for people already in the organization and attracts desirable recruits. Decision-making is easy, or seems easy, because good decisions are confirmed, and poor decisions are masked, by continuing growth. The decision-maker has a wider range of choices than would be possible in a stable or declining organization.

For the very same reasons, mistakes are likely to be made in the management of a growing organization, even if the mistakes do not show. It is probably harder to run a growing organization really well than to run the same type of organization in a stable phase, and the more rapid the growth, the more difficult the task.

Managerial Problems in Growing Organizations

It is obvious that a manager of given ability can control a small organization more firmly than a large one, supervise more of its activity directly, observe more of what goes on, and understand a larger proportion of the relationships subordinates have with each other and with outsiders. As the organization grows, control becomes more complex by the mere accretion of numbers. There are ways of reducing the complexity by delegating responsibility and installing better data systems, but there is no way of avoiding it altogether.

The diminution of consensus about organizational goals is a normal consequence of growth, attributable in part to the inherent difficulty of getting a larger number of people who know each other less well to agree about anything, in part to the importation of new people and ideas, but mostly to the brute fact that as an organization grows, its relationships to its members and to the environment necessarily change, so that its original goals become less congruent with its current program. These problems are magnified by discontinuities of scale. No organization can grow indefinitely in small increments. Sooner or later it makes a quantum leap that transforms its whole character: a company acquires a second factory in another state; a summer camp adds a winter program; a family has its first child. Often the people involved may not realize that anything significant has occurred until they discover by experience that their familiar procedures no longer work and that their familiar routines have been bizarrely transformed.

One sign of discontinuity is the breakdown of organizational norms. There is a point in the growth of nearly every organization when internal theft becomes a problem and new security measures must be devised. In growing organizations that are badly run, a criminal underground may develop.

The growth of an organization makes some of its people obsolete. Some of its original members—perhaps those who deserve most of the credit for growth—will be unwilling or unable to adjust to the new order, and will be left by the wayside.

While the growing organization discards some of its insiders, its dependence on outsiders increases, because the expanded program requires transactions with an expanded environment or because growth has been achieved by mortgaging resources or assuming long-term commitments. Most successful private enterprises in the United States have gone this route, sacrificing independence for growth and eventually falling under the control of outside investors.

The problems of managing a growing organization are not insurmountable, but they do become more severe as the rate of growth accelerates, and organizations that grow very rapidly are often managed so badly that they ultimately collapse.

The standard methods for coping with rapid expansion in an organization (of any size) are:

1. team management,

2. decentralization of operating responsibilities,

3. standardization of procedures,

4. centralization of financial control,

5. improved communication facilities.

This formula, although derived from case studies of organizations of varying size, bears a close resemblance to the Sloan plan for General Motors that we discussed in the third chapter. The resemblance is not coincidental, since the Sloan plan was, in fact, designed for a rapidly expanding organization and worked well for upward of forty years until GM reached a level of relative stability and began to encounter a different set of problems. The same organization that had coped so well with the problems of expansion became remarkably maladroit when asked to cope with consumer activists, federal regulation of engine emissions, and the design constraints introduced by high-priced gasoline.

Although the formula set forth above calls to mind a giant organization, I have seen it applied with notable success to middle-sized and even tiny organizations—a piano company taking on the manufacture of electric organs, a civic orchestra becoming a full-time professional orchestra, a research institute outgrowing the converted barn in which it started.

Under team management, the single, ultimately responsible head of the organization to whom this book is addressed sometimes becomes two or three people who divide the job up or do it jointly.[3] More commonly under team management, the manager of the organization can still be identified but has one or two close associates whose authority is nearly equal to his or her own. The reason for team management in rapidly expanding organizations is that there are at least three separate managerial jobs to be done: running the existing operation, supervising the expansion, and coping with the unpredictable problems that expansion creates.

But since there are built-in limits to the size of a managerial team (no executive committee is likely to function well with more than five members), the continued expansion of an organization continuously threatens to overload the management team unless the responsibility for routine and subsidiary operations is spun off as soon as possible to subordinate managers. Hence the need for decentralization. Decentralization is only feasible, however, if procedures are standardized and financial controls are tightened; otherwise it amounts to anarchy. When decentralization has been accomplished, there remains the danger that the organization's ability to react to events as a unit will suffer because its decentralized parts lack a common viewpoint. Hence the need for improved communications.

Managerial Problems in Stable Organizations

By a stable organization, I mean one that is not growing or declining significantly. It need not be stable in all other respects.

Some organizations are inherently stable because they are designed to operate with a membership of fixed size—a troupe of aerialists, for example, or a string quartet, or a state legislature. Some, such as the Central Mental Hospital described by Erving Goffman in his notable book on asylums,[4] must confine their activities to fixed facilities, and therefore have approximately stable populations.

Some other organizations are stable by deliberate choice, steering a careful course between the temptation to grow and the danger of declining. A considerable number of small communities and small associations are run this way, and even a few sizable businesses. One Great Lakes shipping line, for example, operated the same fleet of eleven bulk carriers out of the same port for a period of thirty-two years, spanning the entire career of one fleet manager, without adding or losing a single ship and without ever replacing a captain for any reason but retirement. The Comédie Française, the French National Theater, has maintained an approximately constant membership for more than three hundred years. It is a cooperative headed by the actor of longest service. A new recruit becomes an associate member after a year's probation and a formal debut in a role of his or her choice but cannot become a *sociétaire* until a vacancy is created by the resignation or death of a member.[5]

As a general rule, morale is higher in stable organizations than in either growing or declining ones, but that is not to say that the stable organization is free of problems. There is the constant problem of assuring that the measures taken to prevent growth do not overcarry and lead into a spiral of decline. Stable organizations tend to be inflexible and set in their ways, and since they generally have low turnover they are apt to become more inflexible as their members age. The ragged, long-bearded crew of the Flying Dutchman's ship, as described in the old sea legend, were not unlike the personnel of some other organizations that have been stable for a long time. A middle-aged colleague of mine who joined the staff of a famous and extremely stable scientific institute in Paris said that he felt conspicuous at staff meetings because he was the only person there without a hearing aid.

Because of their built-in resistance to change, stable organizations are vulnerable to certain types of crisis. Crises of succession, when they occur in stable organizations, are especially severe, since career frustration in a stable organization is a more serious matter than in a dynamic organization. I knew a man who served for seventeen years as the associate director of a stable industrial laboratory, secure in the knowledge that when the director reached the mandatory retirement age, the place would be his, and that he would then have fourteen more years to run the laboratory before his own retirement. In due course, the director retired and, to everybody's surprise, a younger man from outside was selected for the post. My friend's reactions were violent, running from initial shock into a nearly suicidal depression that required him to take a long leave of absence. When he recovered, he returned to work in his old job, with the fixed intention of taking revenge at the first opportunity. As it turned out, the new director was sufficiently incompetent to fail even without my friend's assistance. Between them, they wrecked the organization beyond repair within two years.

Such disasters are avoidable provided that the stable organization refrains from actions—such as disrupting an orderly succession—that are incompatible with long-term stability. Some Oxford and Cambridge colleges have remained stable for centuries. The best account of how such an organization handles a crisis of succession may be found, lightly disguised as fiction, in C. P. Snow's novel *The Masters,* in which the fellows of a Cambridge college, selecting their new head in a bitterly contested election, take elaborate account of the motives and expectations of all concerned in order to arrive at the least disruptive choice.

The principal elements of the formula for managing a stable organization are these:

1. adherence to traditional procedures,

2. slow-moving, intensive problem-solving efforts,

3. democratic participation in decision-making,

4. meticulous and accessible records and accounts,

5. a system for the designation of successors designed to prevent surprises.

A stable organization cannot be maintained for long unless it has the wholehearted support of its members and they keep a vigilant lookout for incipient signs of growth or decline. In order for the organization to obtain that much support from its members, it must assure that their expectations are rarely disappointed, and in order to do that, it must follow a slow participatory mode of problem-solving. The manager of a stable organization is less of an initiator and more of a representative than the managers of growing and declining organizations, and your success as a manager of a stable organization is measured by how well you express the wishes of your constituents.

Managerial Problems in Declining Organizations

Organizations decline for a variety of reasons, not all of which signify failure. A few types of organization have a built-in, normal rate of decline. An organized alumnae group, like the Old Ivy class of 1985, begins its existence with a maximum roster and declines over the years as members die or are lost from sight, until the roster is emptied seventy or eighty years later. Veterans' organizations follow a similar course. Some very important types of organization anticipate cyclical decline as a matter of course. Standing armies and navies grow rapidly in wartime and decline even faster when the war comes to an end. Some organizations are plunged into a decline by achieving their original goals. The associations formed to combat tuberculosis and poliomyelitis are classic, much-studied examples.

Tax-supported agencies decline when their appropriations are reduced. Schools, hospitals, and other service institutions decline when shifts of population reduce the demand for their services. A commercial enterprise may decline because of shrinking markets. The producers of washtubs, laundry soap, blueing, and other materials for doing laundry by hand have sold their products in a shrinking market for decades since the invention of washing machines.

As a general rule, it is much more difficult to manage a declining organization than a stable or growing one. The growing organization is rarely confronted by a truly insoluble problem—there is usually some way around it. The stable organization has learned to keep insoluble problems at bay, or it would not be stable. But the declining organization has problems that cannot be solved.

Morale is usually low in declining organizations. Because of the organization's diminishing ability to meet its commitments, it must often disappoint the legitimate expectations of its members. In addition, they experience an automatic status deflation as the organization's importance diminishes and the importance of their own activities is correspondingly reduced. When the decline of an organization is unscheduled, there is certain to be some loss of confidence in its program; this is likely to occur even when the decline is scheduled. Few professional groups are less certain of their own purposes than the officers of a peacetime army. This loss of confidence breeds cynicism and encourages corruption. Declining organizations are susceptible to exploitation by outsiders, and to looting by their own members.

The productivity of declining organizations is typically low because of inadequate resources to keep up with technological progress and the difficulty of recruiting competent replacements when positions fall vacant.

A specific malady that afflicts declining organizations may be called "Parkinsonitis," after the brilliant satirist who invented Parkinson's Law.[6] Its leading symptom is the expansion of administrative overhead as the operations contract. In a case of Parkinsonitis, the number of administrators and the costs of administration actually increase with each decrease in the number of people and activities to be administered. Parkinson presented figures for the Royal Navy between 1914 and 1928. During that period, the number of capital ships in commission decreased by 68 percent and the number of naval personnel by 32 percent, while the number of Admiralty officials *increased* by 78 percent. Another set of figures presented in the same essay showed a nearly fourfold increase in the staff of the British Colonial Office between 1935 and 1954, during which period the colonial empire administered by that office was liquidated. More recently, John Freeman and Michael T. Hannon have demonstrated the existence of Parkinsonitis in California school districts with an elaborate mathematical model.[7]

The new manager of a declining organization starts with two strikes against him. First, he is sure to find numerous deficiencies. Second, the chance of ultimate success is poor. Nevertheless, even declining organizations need to be managed, and there is the consoling thought that failure in the management of a declining organization is not much of a disgrace, while success is a notable achievement.

The formula for managing a declining organization may be summarized as follows:

1. reduce administrative overhead at a faster rate than the shrinkage of other activities,

2. drop the nonessential parts of the organizational program,

3. identify the inefficient and corrupt units and eliminate them,

4. when the organization has been stripped of its nonessential functions and purged of its worst abuses, look for new activities and goals.

Adjusting to Market Pressures

Aside from the permanent decline that leads to extinction, every healthy organization is susceptible to temporary phases of decline due to competition, scarcities, rising costs, or declining revenues.

Competition

Every organization in the world competes with other organizations for resources, influence, manpower, and clients. Most organizations are simultaneously pitted against several distinct sets of competitors. A manufacturer of table linen competes, of course, with other linen manufacturers but also with linen importers; with manufacturers of paper napkins, plastic tablecloths, place mats, and disposable fabrics; and with commercial linen services and discount houses that buy linen from captive suppliers.

A noncommercial institution also has separate sets of competitors. A private liberal arts college, for example, competes intensely and consciously with other colleges in its league—those of about the same size and type in the same region, but it is also willy-nilly in competition with publicly supported institutions from state universities down to community colleges, and with alternative institutions such as vocational schools and service academies.

When market conditions are highly favorable, competitive efforts are directed almost exclusively against nearby competitors—against the other middle-size manufacturers of fine table linen, or against the other second-rank New England women's colleges. When market conditions turn unfavorable, the competitive focus shifts to more remote but more threatening competitors: the paper goods industry, the community colleges. The most successful competitors are generally those who are able to see a coming change of competitive focus earlier than their peers.

Scarcities

The most dangerous kind of market pressure is an absolute scarcity of something the organization requires for its program. A relative scarcity of material or manpower will be reflected, of course, in rising costs, and a relative scarcity of clients and customers will take the form of declining revenues. An absolute scarcity is a different sort of problem, and not particularly uncommon.

An absolute scarcity occurs when, for example, the balsa wood used for model planes is no longer available because of a trade embargo; the county hospital cannot be staffed because physicians' services have been priced out of reach; the Sunday school must be abandoned because the congregation has few young children; the municipal auditorium is condemned after a fire and there is no other hall large enough for the civic orchestra's concerts; the abandonment of air service to an island resort keeps all the tourists away; the exhaustion of the silver lode closes down the mine and the mining town.

An absolute scarcity cannot be argued with or fiddled with. It calls for imaginative and *quick* innovation, before the organization founders.

Rising Costs

Rising costs may reflect the appearances of relative scarcities, as when a poor flax crop raises the price of linen or a shortage of psychological counselors increases the salaries that must be offered to hire one. But there are many other reasons why costs rise, some of them internal to the organization, such as ineffective administration, worn-out equipment, or embezzlement; some of them external, such as new taxes, increased postal rates, or inflation. Some of these factors raise costs gradually, but others work abruptly so that, for example, every rise in fourth-class postage rates spells the end for some magazines, and every extension of minimum-wage coverage puts a stop to various small enterprises. The effect of rising costs is most dramatic when the organization is not free to pass on increases to its customers or clients. But even when it is, there comes a point where further increases reduce revenues. That is the problem that faces private liberal arts colleges. Their tuition fees are already very high in relation to the ability of students' families to pay, and further increases to meet rising costs drive so many students away to publicly supported institutions that total revenues decline. Urban mass-transit systems have been caught in a similar spiral for many years. Increasing costs of labor, fuel, and equipment force them to increase their fares periodically, but every increase reduces the number of passengers, which soon calls for a further increase of fares, which reduces the number of passengers still more, and so on down the spiral of insolvency. The fundamental remedy for rising costs due to inflation is technological improvement, and the usual remedy for rising costs due to government intervention is lobbying, but these measures are not necessarily effective. The liberal arts college cannot introduce much technological improvement without changing its institutional character and losing much of its remaining clientele, and the operators of urban bus lines can bring only a limited influence to bear on government policy.

Declining Revenues

Declining revenues have much the same effect as rising costs, but in the typical case they are a little more under the organization's control, since the decline can sometimes be arrested by vigorous cultivation of an existing clientele or by reaching out for new clients. Advertising and promotion offer the commercial enterprise innumerable opportunities to turn declining sales trends around. Intelligent programs of attracting students enable some liberal arts colleges to flourish when most are declining. Hospitals, churches, schools, clubs, civic associations, and innumerable other organizations that depend on voluntary support are often able to reverse a declining revenue trend by intensive cultivation of their existing constituencies, or by reaching out for new supporters.

Responding to Market Pressures

The formula for responding to market pressure may be briefly summarized as follows:

1. *Remember that no trend lasts forever.* The time of peace is the time to prepare for war, and the time of increasing revenue is the time to plan and prepare for a phase of declining revenue.

2. *Every technological improvement should be justified by cost reduction.* Technological improvements are possible in nearly every organized human activity, but since it is also possible to burden nearly any activity with new devices that are not really needed, a technological improvement should not be adopted unless it offers a significant cost benefit.

3. *Make multiple responses to market pressure whenever possible, and determine by trial and error which responses are most effective.* An organization's response to market pressure is affected not only by unpredictable fluctuations of the market but also by the reactions of competitors. This field of action resembles a storm at sea more than it resembles a field to be plowed and planted. To get through it safely, you need to stand by your instruments, take continuous readings, and be prepared to change course frequently.

Adjusting to Social Change

No organization can be completely insulated from the currents of social change in the surrounding society. And all societies change continually—not only advanced, industrial societies but *all* societies. The changes that occur in our own society can be classified in many different ways, but those that have the most impact on organizations fall conveniently into four categories: demographic shifts, changes of public policy, changes in social values, and changes in organizational styles.

Demographic Shifts

Demographic shifts occur because of the growth or decline of population in a given territory, or changing rates of growth or decline; because of migration from country to city, from central city to suburb, and from region to region; because of fluctuations in birthrates, death rates, and other vital statistics; and because of the changes in the age, sex, ethnicity, and other characteristics of given populations that are induced by all of the foregoing processes.

Every demographic shift has some effect on organizations, and some of these effects ripple on for decades. For example, the rise in the United States birthrate that occurred in the late 1940s necessitated a great expansion of elementary schools in the 1950s, of high schools a little later, and of colleges and universities in the 1960s. The sharp decline of the same birthrate that occurred in the 1970s calls for a shrinkage of educational institutions in the 1980s that will continue at least until the end of the century.

To take another familiar example, the migration of urban dwellers to the suburbs has profound effects upon the city churches they formerly attended, which respond to the problem of declining attendance and interest in a variety of ways. Some urban churches follow their congregations to the suburbs. Some continue to operate on a much reduced scale for a remnant of elderly parishioners, some go out of existence, and some reorganize to serve a new clientele.

No national population in the modern world has a fixed size, distribution, or composition; all of them are continuously changing. Hence, all modern organizations are subject to continuous demographic shifts that change the number and type of people available for participation in their programs.

Changes of Public Policy

Changes in public policy have frequent and unpredictable effects upon organizations of every kind in every modern society. In the People's Democracies, no aspect of organizational life falls outside the sphere of official control. Under a freer form of government, the jurisdiction of the state is more limited, but the expenditures of all levels of government in the United States account for more than a third of the gross national product, and governmental control over nongovernmental organizations is expressed by an unending stream of statutes, regulations, and rulings emitted by legislatures, courts, and administrative agencies. Even the most private association, like a fishing club, must file a tax statement, apply for licenses, conform to health, safety, and zoning regulations, pay minimum wages, refrain from illegal discrimination, operate equipment in a prescribed manner, and so on and so forth. An establishment of a more public character, like a hospital, operates within an intricate maze of government controls.

There are hundreds of separate government bodies with the power to alter some of the public policies that control the operation of a hospital, and many of them are hyperactive in developing new policies and procedures. For example, in the reimbursement of hospitals for patient charges from public funds, about the only thing that can be taken for granted concerning the policies and procedures in effect at a given time is that they will not be the same twelve months later.

A statute or court ruling intended to accomplish some unrelated purpose may transform an organization's environment beyond recognition, as has frequently happened in recent years to organizations as diverse as nursery schools, nursing homes, and tree nurseries, within my own observation. In the case of the nursery schools, a careless phrase in a state law on the licensing of schoolteachers had the effect of requiring nursery schoolteachers to have bachelor's degrees in education, thereby eliminating a good proportion of the nursery schools in that state and tripling the average charges of those that remained. In the case of nursing homes, a small change in the regulations concerning Medicare eligibility forced large nursing homes to dismantle their facilities for intensive medical care. In the case of the tree nurseries, a minor revision in the tax regulations concerning depletion allowances made Christmas tree nurseries highly attractive to investors at one time, while another minor revision some years later made them instantly unprofitable.

In the great expansion of federal jurisdiction that began around 1964 and continued until 1980, many activities that were already regulated by state and local agencies were brought under federal jurisdiction as well. At the same time, federal agencies with somewhat contradictory mandates, like the Department of Energy and the EPA, devised innumerable regulations that took little account of the regulations of competing agencies. Lending institutions, elementary schools, trucklines, hospitals, pharmaceutical manufacturers, automobile manufacturers, racetracks, food distributors, express services now have to cope with ten to twenty regulatory agencies whose requirements are sometimes redundant, incoherent, or flatly contradictory and always impose a considerable burden of recordkeeping and other paperwork.[8] The organization that tries to cope with government regulation in an imaginative way and the manager who devotes much time to regulatory matters are both asking for trouble. Conforming to burdensome regulations—or for that matter, evading them—is a matter for experts, for accountants, lawyers, and other professionals who specialize in such matters. Enterprises that deal with regulatory agencies through an intermediary body like a trade association have a much easier time of it than those that attempt to deal directly with government agencies and improvise their responses to regulatory pressure.

The realm of public policy constitutes a Pandora's box of unexpected surprises, sometimes pleasant but more often unpleasant for the modern organization. Nearly every sizable organization is continually engaged in lobbying and litigation, either directly or through representative associations. Nevertheless, since changes in public policy come from so many different quarters, an organization will often be unaware that some significant modification is about to be required in its program until the change is upon it. The Buckley amendment requiring educational institutions to give students access to confidential records about themselves, which transformed the record-keeping procedures of educational institutions, was enacted and took effect before the affected institutions or their official lobbyists were aware that such a measure was pending.

Changes in Social Values

Changes in social values are even more unpredictable in the long run than changes in public policy, but since they are much less abrupt, they permit more planning and adaptation. Changes in social values involve such matters as the relationship between the sexes, the attitudes of young people toward their elders, the limits of legitimate authority, the recognition or denial of property rights, the importance attached to education and to leisure, the role of religion in daily life, the tolerance accorded to people of different color or descent, and the definition of what constitutes acceptable appearance, speech, and behavior in various settings. No organization is impermeable to changes in social values, but most organizations do not absorb such changes passively; they either encourage or resist them. With respect to such a matter as the equalization of sex roles, a strong organization is likely to be either far ahead of, or far behind, the general social trend. Few organizations, however, remain unaffected.

Changes in Organizational Styles

Organizational styles change as frequently as styles in clothing or entertainment. Fashions and fads in organizational matters are partly derived from the external environment and partly self-generated. Modern organizations of any one type stay in close touch through conventions and periodicals, so that any significant innovation in an organization is noticed almost immediately by other organizations in the same set, and any innovation that has been adopted by a number of organizations in a set becomes almost irresistible to the others. A bank without a computer, or a church without a revised liturgy, would be a rarity today, although the advantage of either innovation is open to question.

When your organization is confronted with an external social change that invites or compels action, you ought to be mindful of the following rules:

1. *Do not be taken unaware.* It is the manager's personal responsibility to be aware of changes in the external environment that affect the organization's program, and this responsibility can never really be delegated.

2. *Do not allow the organization to react hastily.* The problems of adjusting an organization to external change are inherently complex, and the probability of finding the right solution is necessarily low.

3. *Specify the end condition to be achieved and then work backward step-by-step to find the appropriate means.* This is known as the sequential method of solving social problems; I have described it in detail in another book.[9]

4. *Make sure that you have a substantial consensus within the organization before responding to external changes.* The existence of a consensus is ascertained by consultation with the people directly or indirectly affected by the proposed course of action. If there is no consensus, it must be developed by having the same people study the problem until they arrive at agreement (or, in extreme circumstances, by a drastic reorganization). How much consensus is enough is always a good question, but it is easy to underestimate the resistance to change that can be mustered by a disgruntled minority, or by the one wicked witch not invited to the christening.

5. *When following organizational fashions, do not be the last with the old nor the first with the new.* This is an old doctor's adage concerning the application of new remedies. It rests on the common-

sense observation that the first users of a new remedy are the ones most likely to suffer from its unknown side effects, while the last users have the least benefit.

Adjusting to Technological Progress

In an advanced technological society, all organizations, including those that have nothing to do with industrial production, are offered a continuous stream of technologically improved devices. The museum of antique furniture is offered a computerized catalog system. The rowing club can pace its practice sessions with an electronically activated timer and can substitute fiberglass oars for wooden ones.

From the technological standpoint, an improvement is an improvement; even the casual observer can usually determine which of two related devices is more advanced along the vector of technological progress. But the problem of whether an organization needs, wants, or can make use of a given bit of new technology is not so easily resolved. It is possible to automate a dairy farm so that the cows are fed and milked without any human intervention, but it is not economically practical to do so except with a very large herd.

From the organizational standpoint, technological improvement usually involves both advantages and disadvantages. The advantages are along the lines of greater speed, scope, capacity, and precision and (sometimes) lower unit costs. The disadvantages are along the lines of the loss of autonomy, waste of skills, reduction in cooperative effort, decreased control, and (sometimes) increased unit costs.

Hence, the adjustment of an organization to technological progress in its field involves two separate tasks: first, choosing or rejecting new technological improvements as they are offered; second, incorporating whatever improvements are chosen into the organizational program with minimum damage. In many technically oriented organizations, there is the third task of contributing to the development of new technology by research and experimentation.

Choosing or Rejecting New Technology

This task is more of a pitfall for small organizations than for large ones. Large organizations, with their specialized technical facilities, participate directly in the current of ongoing research and usually have rational procedures for appraising the advantages and disadvantages of a proposed bit of new technology. There are some notable exceptions, however. The U.S. Postal Service, for example, has so powerful a tradition of technological ineptness that private message and parcel services are able to compete with it effectively, despite the enormous subsidy it enjoys.

In any case, the rules of thumb for choosing or rejecting a new bit of technology are the same for organizations of every size. They may be summarized as follows:

1. Adopt a technological improvement when it offers a large reduction of cost, or an unmistakable gain of effectiveness without any increased cost.

2. Reject a technological improvement when its effects on cost or effectiveness are uncertain.

3. Adopt a technological improvement if it can be introduced on an experimental basis without serious jeopardy to the organizational program in case of failure.

4. Reject a technological improvement that exposes the organization to disaster in case of failure.

Incorporating New Technology into an Organization

The decision to adopt a new bit of technology is frequently made at the top level of an organization (or by outsiders, in the case of organizations that are components of larger ones) without any serious attention to the problem of fitting the innovation into the organization. That is where the sociological fun begins.

The installation of a new bit of technology in an organization bears some resemblance to the modernization of a primitive village by well-meaning outside experts. The things that can go wrong because the experts fail to take full account of the customs and beliefs of the natives were admirably cataloged by Conrad Arensberg and Arthur Niehoff in the manual they prepared for American experts working overseas.

They had many anecdotes to tell about misdirected technological improvements; for example, in Laotian villages, Leghorn and Rhode Island Red roosters were put into village flocks to raise a more productive mixed breed:

Some American chickens survived but even these got no chance to prove their usefulness. They rarely were able to mate with the local hens because they were no match for the gamecocks that served as roosters in the local flocks. The chicken expert tried to get around this difficulty by demanding that a villager get rid of all of his local roosters before he would put some American ones in the flock. This worked for one generation. Then the sons of the American roosters and the Lao hens took over. Being half village chicken, they were tougher fighters than their fathers, and kept the latter from mating. In this manner, each generation became inferior in size and egg-producing ability, but superior in fighting.[10]

The reason that the American expert could not overcome these difficulties was that he never fully visualized the difference between the American system of raising chickens in a tightly controlled hen house environment and the Laotian system of letting the chickens forage for themselves, nor did he perceive the connection between cock-fighting and poultry raising.

Exactly the same sort of incomprehension often attends the introduction of a technological innovation in a sophisticated enterprise. A textbook publisher who installed an automated shipping system in a computerized warehouse discovered that his salesmen were ordering out huge numbers of examination copies under fictitious names and hoarding them. The new system, it turned out, had an average delivery time of around fifteen days, much less than that of the previous system; but, unlike the previous system, it was incapable of delivering a book overnight on a salesman's rush order. Since the salesmen depended on such rush orders whenever a buyer showed interest, they bypassed the new warehouse and improvised a makeshift system of their own in order to get their work done.

What appears to be an irrational resistance to technology often turns out, on closer analysis, to be rational enough from the standpoint of the resisters. The Lancaster weavers who smashed the power looms at the very beginning of the Industrial Revolution feared that their wages would be lowered by the new invention and they were perfectly right.

Even when the resistance to an invention is irrational, it may be quite reasonable in terms of the information available to the resisters. The fault in such cases lies with the innovators for not having sufficiently studied the environment in which they proposed to operate.

To take another example from the modernization of developing countries, the team of agronomists from the University of Iowa who attempted to introduce an improved variety of seed corn in highland Guatemala discovered that, although the local farmers took the corn gratefully enough, they fed it to their animals instead of planting it. After two or three seasons of this charade, the agronomists, on the advice of an astute Indian, put a high fence studded with No Trespassing signs around their compound and stopped giving their seed corn away. But they left the fence unguarded at night and enough corn was stolen and planted to establish the new variety. In that part of the world, nearly every family has its own subvariety of corn, and it is much too valuable to give away. But if it appears really superior, the neighbors will pilfer some to try out.

The first series of experiments at the Western Electric plant in Hawthorne more than half a century ago, which had such a profound effect on the development of industrial sociology, attempted to demonstrate the effect of improved lighting on the productivity of factory work groups. In one of these experiments, a test group was chosen to work under progressively improving illumination. It was carefully matched with a control group, working under constant illumination. The results were startling. The increase of productivity in the control group was nearly the same as the increase in the experimental group. In a follow-up experiment, both the test group and the control group were placed in artificial light, and this time the level of illumination in the test group enclosure was gradually decreased. Again, the efficiencies of the test group and the control group increased at about the same rate. Not until the test group's illumination was reduced to the approximate brightness of moonlight, so that they could barely see their materials, did output begin to decrease.

The implication of this experiment was that the level of illumination had only a minor influence on productivity in that particular setting, but that the amount of supervisory attention received by a work group had a major influence. Both the test group and the control group were closely watched, fussed over, and consulted by supervisors during the course of the experiment; the favorable effects of this increased attention overcame the minor effects of varying illumination.

In general, the successful introduction of a technological innovation depends upon predicting with reasonable accuracy (1) what functions the innovation will perform and how these will affect the organization's structure, and (2) obtaining—preferably in advance—the consent and cooperation of the people who are expected to make the innovation work.

The usual procedures for accomplishing these purposes may be summarized as follows:

1. Before committing the organization to a technological innovation, it is essential to obtain empirical evidence that the innovation is workable, by means of a pilot installation or by close observation of a comparable organization in which it is already operational.

2. The more people involved in preliminary discussion of, and planning for, the innovation, the more successful it is likely to be.

3. When resistance to an innovation begins to develop, stop the clock and resolve the problem before proceeding further. Resistance of this kind should not be approached as an obstacle to be surmounted. It may be solidly grounded on technical or social facts that need to be taken into account.

4. Try to determine in advance, primarily by consultation outside and inside the organization, the probable defects of a proposed innovation so as to be prepared to cope with them as they appear.

5. A technological innovation should be monitored for a considerable period of time after its installation in order to detect those malfunctions that take some time to develop and in order to measure the results of the innovation when it settles into a steady state of operation.

Creative Innovation

March and Simon, in their classic treatise on the theory of organization, hypothesize that "most innovations in an organization are a result of borrowing rather than invention."[11] The borrowing is accomplished either by direct imitation of other organizations or by importing people who have experience elsewhere. The practice of borrowing makes eminent good sense, particularly for small organizations, since the borrower is spared the cost of invention and testing and is protected from the error in trial and error.

Nevertheless, any organization may occasionally invent a new technical or social device, and some organizations specialize in creative innovation. This activity is undertaken with varying degrees of seriousness in scientific laboratories, research and development teams, advertising agencies, law firms, and a few high-level planning agencies.

Under primitive conditions, creative innovation is the exclusive prerogative of a few individuals who have the rare talent of perceiving possibilities to which their fellows are blind. While filming the lives of monkeys (red-faced macaques) on the island of Kochima, a team of Japanese zoologists actually saw a young female, whom they nicknamed Imo, hit on the idea of washing a sweet potato in the lake before eating it. After about a month, she was imitated by another monkey, and ten years later, the practice had spread throughout the band. Later, Imo made a second fundamental discovery when she found a way of separating grain from sand by tossing a pawful of grain on the surface of the water and letting the sand sink. "She was something of a monkey Prometheus," wrote one of the observers.[12]

The characteristics of inventive geniuses do not change very much as we ascend the evolutionary scale. They are rare, conscious of their special gifts, and capable of making multiple discoveries under the right conditions. Creative innovators seem to have distinctive mental and personality traits. They rate high on conceptual fluency and flexibility, respond to stimuli in original and atypical ways, and enjoy complex problems. They are likely to be stubborn about their opinions, somewhat lonely, impulsive, and resistant to authority. In other words, they are not good executive material.[13]

The question of how to design an organization to encourage and facilitate creative innovation cannot, in the present state of knowledge, be answered by a formula. There is considerable disagreement among successful research administrators about how much autonomy the creative innovator needs to have. The question is complicated by the fact that in contemporary science, technology, and social management, the problems to be solved by creative innovation sometimes call for massive team efforts. The individual capable of original discoveries does not lose his or her importance, but the innovator's work must now be coordinated with the less original efforts of numerous hardworking collaborators.

The available research evidence suggests that administrative style, tables of organization, and operating procedures are less important in creative organizations than in those with more routine programs. The most productive research organization I have ever observed was Millard Hansen's Social Science Research Center at the University of Puerto Rico—although it was enmeshed in the toils of an old-fashioned, slow-moving, bilingual bureaucracy. The secret of the center's success seems to have been that project directors were very carefully selected and then given unlimited responsibility for their projects and as much support as the center could provide with no questions asked and few reports required. The classic prototype of the American industrial laboratory, the research division of General Electric under Irving Langmuir, operated in a similar fashion.

On the other hand, the two greatest achievements of American technology, the Manhattan project and the NASA moon program, were carried out by tightly administered organizations, each of which had a rather narrow and rigid division of labor. In contrast to the absence of deadlines in Hansen's center and Langmuir's laboratory (other than those self-imposed by individuals), some effective research organizations not only impose deadlines but use the trick of a suddenly advanced deadline to achieve breakthroughs on stubborn problems.

While the optimum design for a creative organization cannot be completely specified, there are a few well-established principles for managing a creative organization, which may be stated as follows:

1. Identify the creative individuals on whom the success of the organization depends, on the basis of their demonstrated performance.

2. Make sure that you and they share a common view of the organization's goals, whether broadly or narrowly defined.

3. Provide them with all the support the organization can muster.

4. Protect them from bureaucratic interference.

5. Reward them as lavishly as possible.

It is obvious from the foregoing that the noncreative people in a creative organization will suffer from relative deprivation, and that the creative people will sometimes get in each other's way. Successful research organizations are seldom characterized by high morale, but that matters little if they are able to make new discoveries.

Systematic Planning

If you have had any organizational experience at all, you will not have needed this book to learn that management is more an art than a science, although the findings of social science may assist us in practicing the art. You would not have needed a book, either, to learn that both pleasures and pains are associated with the headship of anything. "Is it not passing brave to be a King and ride in triumph through Persepolis?" asked Christopher Marlowe in *Tamburlaine.* "Uneasy lies the head that wears a crown," his greater contemporary wrote in *Henry IV.*

The principles of conduct proposed in the foregoing pages can be read backward as signposts pointing toward the pitfalls into which a manager may fall, and sometimes *must* fall. The balance between success and failure in running an organization is so delicate that common sense tells us to count no manager successful until he or she has retired and gone away.

Is there some sure method of tipping this uncertain balance in our favor? The answer is *no* if we want to be guaranteed against unknown dangers, unprovoked hostility, and the consequences of our own mistakes. The answer is *yes* if we want to maintain authority, encourage communication, achieve high levels of productivity and morale, and adapt successfully to change. A nearly magical enhancement of a manager's personal capability can be achieved nine times out of ten by an intelligent emphasis on planning.

In nearly every kind of organization, the manager has a primary responsibility for planning that is not likely to be questioned or disputed.[14] Even a manager with very limited authority, like the principal of a public school or the president of a civic association, is usually free to launch as much planning activity as he or she wants and can enlist others in a planning program without meeting much resistance.

Not all of what passes for organizational planning deserves the name. Some so-called plans are really sales prospectuses. Others are science fiction. In a few interesting cases, the sole function of planning is to direct attention away from the real problems. Serious planning, by contrast, is marked by an emphasis on contingency and by a meticulous interest in small details.

Planning may, of course, be short term, middle term, or long term; routine or episodic; problem-oriented or goal-oritented; participant or nonparticipant. But the essential features of a well-conceived planning program are not very much affected by these distinctions. They are as follows:

1. A detailed description of the current state of the organization and of the relevant features of the environment.

2. An analysis of past trends in the organization and in the envi-

ronment to provide a basis for extrapolating the same trends into the future.

3. A division of the future into a sequence of successive stages and a description of the conditions to be achieved at each stage.

4. Estimates of the organizational inputs required to move from each stage to the next of the planned sequence.

5. Specification of the external conditions required to carry the plan through its successive stages.

6. A method for measuring plan fulfillment at each stage.

7. Provisions for revising the plan in case of overfulfillment, underfulfillment, or unforeseen contingencies.

The direct advantages of planning are obvious. The indirect benefits are not quite so obvious but they are just as real and just as important.

Self-Appraisal

In organizations that practice continuous short-term planning, for example, in companies that set production or sales quotas for six months or a year ahead, the pressures for achievement on the one hand, and the politics of quota-setting on the other hand, force every unit of the organization—down to the individual worker—to practice continuous self-appraisal. In middle- and long-term planning, a major planning episode usually begins with a self-survey in which units assess their past progress, present performance, and potential capability in relation to the organization's stated goals. This experience, repeated at reasonable intervals and in a reasonably democratic spirit, has all sorts of wonderful side effects. It is by far the most effective way of clarifying the organization's purposes and bringing the activities of component units into alignment with them. It leads units to uncover and resolve many structural and operating problems that would otherwise go untreated. It elicits information and suggestions from sectors of the organization that do not normally play much part in formulating policy, while the need to combine the reports of lower units at each level provokes intense communication—upward, downward, and sideways—about organizational problems.[15]

Clarification of Goals

No matter how clearly the initial goals of an organization are stated or understood, some ambiguities, differences of opinion, and misunderstandings are sure to develop in the course of normal operations, with the result that one part of the program pulls against another, or some units spend their energies undoing the work of other units. Planning brings these contradictions to light and provides incentives to resolve them, at least within the confines of the plan.[16]

New Possibilities

Part of the magic of planning is the inevitable discovery of possible courses of action not previously imagined or noticed. The simple procedure of arranging alternatives and contingencies in an orderly way often leads to useful new strategies that would not otherwise have been suggested.

Improved Information

Nearly the first thing that happens in the preparation of an organizational plan is that people find they need information that is not readily available, either because the reporting system is not set up to deliver it, or because it has not been collected, or because it needs to be obtained from outside the organization. When the reporting system has been modified to produce the needed information, or channels to outside sources of information have been established, there is likely to be a permanent improvement in the flow of routine information.

How Not to Plan

Planning, like any other magic, can turn against its user. The failures of planning loom so large in the current world that they deserve separate consideration. Defective planning is one of the hallmarks of modern bureaucracy; it takes several familiar forms:

1. *Setting organizational objectives without participation and consent.* This is the characteristic form of planning in the Soviet economy and, to a lesser extent, in the other centralized economies

of eastern Europe. It is one of the principal reasons why their productivity lags so far behind that of the partially planned economies of western Europe, despite the advantage of more tightly disciplined labor forces in the eastern countries.

2. *Planning with unlimited resources.* The whole point of planning is that it enables an organization to adjust its program to existing constraints in a realistic way. Limited resources constitute the fundamental constraint in most cases. If, for some reason, the resources potentially available to an organization are limited only by its demands, there will be a tendency to plan for maximum growth rather than maximum effectiveness. This is a common occurrence in government agencies when they draw on resources that, at least in the short and middle term, are virtually unlimited. It occurs also in some private organizations whose budgets are so small in relation to the sources from which they draw support as to be practically unlimited. For example, the private security forces of large private institutions seem to develop in a less effective way when planned than when unplanned, since the planning of security services is conventionally oriented toward expansion rather than efficiency.

3. *Master planning.* Master planning is an aberration of the planning process to which American communities are particularly susceptible. The preparation of a master plan is a gigantic effort, altogether out of scale with routine planning activities. The typical master plan is not a statement of intentions but a mixture of practical possibilities and pious hopes that refer to some future time too remote to be controlled from the present. In many cases, the master plan takes so long to prepare that it is outdated before it is published. Master plans seldom specify intermediate stages in detail and, because of their gigantic scale, are not easily amended to take account of intervening events. But the overhanging presence of a master plan has a tendency to inhibit or interfere with realistic planning on a smaller scale.

4. *Planning by outsiders.* It is a common practice for large-scale organizations of every kind to bring in outside experts to do their long-term planning. In some instances where the plan involves very little besides the installation of a new technology, as in the construction of a water purification plant, this procedure makes sense. In the more usual situation, in which modifications in the structure or functions of a living organization are contemplated, it is nearly impossible for outsiders to plan effectively, however knowledgeable and experienced they may be. Consultants are useful to get the planning process going, to suggest new methods and new systems, and to carry

styles of self-improvement from one organization to another; but they cannot successfully plan the future of an organization to which they do not belong. That is the inherent responsibility of the organization's active members. Without their consent and participation, planning is a hollow show.

How to Phase Yourself Out

Involvement in long-term planning serves to remind you that your tenure of office will not be eternal and forces you to consider the relationship between your policies and those of your successor, a subject you might otherwise be tempted to overlook.

In very large organizations, the problem of arranging an orderly succession, and of striking a balance between the continuity of policy that is so desirable and the fresh start that every successor is entitled to make, is not likely to be overlooked. A report on the General Electric company states somewhat breathlessly that the chief operating executive "keeps current a list of five potential successors for his job." But in organizations of a more modest scale, and in the many large organizations that operate under the lengthened shadow of one leader, the questions associated with succession commonly come under a kind of primitive taboo. As in some African tribes, he who mentions the death of the chief is suspected of working to bring it about.

Aside from dispelling this taboo, which is in every way unwholesome, the manager who plans his own succession is certain to discover that more is involved than finding a younger man or woman with big enough feet to fill his shoes. In nearly every organization, it is part of managerial responsibility to assure that such a person, or two or three of them, will be available when the time comes, and doing so requires some restructuring of the current program.

In many instances, you will be led to the further discovery that the most effective transition would be gradual and that the selection of a successor ought to take place before—in some cases long before—your own retirement.

When you give serious consideration to the problem of how to establish your successor's authority on a firm basis, you have come full circle and are again confronting the problem with which you started. If you get that far without cynicism or remorse, you and the organization will have done very well by each other.

Notes

Introduction

1. Some interesting evidence for the point made here is presented by David R. James and Michael Sorel, "Managerial Theory: Unmaking of the Corporation President," *American Sociological Review* 46, no. 1 (February 1981):1–18.

Chapter 1

1. Although not always possible. As one textbook of management observes with notable understatement, "If the senior executive is caught between the requirement that he exercise his power and his wish to be liked by his subordinates, he can easily get into difficulty." Harry Levinson and Cynthia Lang, *Executive* (Cambridge, Mass.: Harvard University Press, 1981), p. 226.

2. For other elements of the pattern, see Oscar Grusky, "The effects of succession: a comparative study of military and business organization," in Oscar Grusky and George A. Miller, eds., *The Sociology of Organizations: Basic Studies* (New York: Free Press, 1970), pp. 439–61.

3. Donald B. Trow, "Executive Succession in Small Companies," *Administrative Science Quarterly* 6, no. 2 (September 1961):237–39.

4. Alvin W. Gouldner, *Patterns of Industrial Bureaucracy* (Glencoe, Ill.: Free Press, 1954), especially pp. 70–101.

5. Robert H. Guest, *Organizational Change: The Effect of Successful Leadership* (Homewood, Ill.: Irwin-Dorsey, 1962).

6. Edmund P. Learned and Audrey T. Sproat, *Organization Theory and Policy: Notes for Analysis* (Homewood, Ill.: Richard D. Irwin, Inc., 1966).

7. Michael Crozier, *The Bureaucratic Phenomenon* (Chicago: University of Chicago Press, 1964), pp. 113–14.

8. Rensis Likert, *New Patterns of Management* (New York: McGraw-Hill, 1961).

9. Georges Friedmann, *Le Travail en Miettes* (Paris: Gallimard, 1956).

10. The story of this development is told in "Pioneers in Industrial Sociology," in John Madge, *The Origins of Scientific Sociology* (Glencoe, Ill.: Free Press, 1962), pp. 162–209.

11. Elliott Jaques, *The Changing Culture of a Factory* (New York: Dryden Press, 1952), p. 277.

12. Peter F. Drucker, *Management: Tasks, Responsibilities, Practices* (New York: Harper & Row, 1974), pp. 241–45.

13. Gordon Tullock, *The Politics of Bureaucracy* (Washington, D.C.: Public Affairs Press, 1965), p. 179.

14. William Foote Whyte, *Street Corner Society: The Social Structure of an Italian Slum* (Chicago: University of Chicago Press, 1943).

15. Ervin Goffman, *Relations in Public: Microstudies of the Public Order* (New York: Basic Books, 1971).

16. Reece M. McGee, "A Study in Ambience: The Numerical Analysis of Interaction Groupings in a Large Scale Organization" (Ph.D. diss., University of Minnesota, 1956).

17. Theodore Caplow, *Two Against One: Coalitions in Triads* (Englewood Cliffs, N.J.: Prentice-Hall, 1968).

18. Georg Simmel, *The Sociology of Georg Simmel*, trans. Kurt H. Wolff (Glencoe, Ill.: Free Press, 1950), pp. 165–66.

19. Theodore C. Sorensen, *Kennedy* (New York: Harper & Row, 1965), pp. 679ff.

Chapter 2

1. Chester I. Barnard, *The Functions of the Executive* (Cambridge, Mass.: Harvard University Press, 1938).

2. Stanley E. Seashore and Ephraim Yuchtman, "The Elements of Organizational Performance," in Bernard P. Indik and F. Kenneth Berrien, eds., *People, Groups, and Organizations* (New York: Teachers College Press, 1968), pp. 172–88.

3. Donald Roy, "Efficiency and 'The Fix': Informal Intergroup Relations in a Piecework Machine Shop," *American Journal of Sociology* 60, no. 3 (November 1954): 255–66.

4. Howard Guetzkow et al., *Simulation in International Relations* (Englewood Cliffs, N.J.: Prentice-Hall, 1963).

5. James David Barber, *Power in Committees: An Experiment in the Governmental Process* (Chicago: Rand-McNally, 1966).

6. Richard F. Fenno, Jr., "The House Appropriations Committee as a Political System: The Problem of Integration," *American Political Science Review* 66 (1962):310–24.

7. Leonard Berkowitz, "Group standards, cohesiveness and productivity," *Human Relations* 7, no. 4 (1954):509–19.

8. F. J. Roethlisberger and William J. Dickson (with Harold A. Wright), *Management and the Worker* (Cambridge, Mass.: Harvard University Press, 1939).

9. A. J. M. Sykes, "A Study in Changing the Attitudes and Stereotypes of Industrial Workers," *Human Relations* 17, no. 2 (1964).

10. Rensis Likert, *New Patterns of Management* (New York: McGraw-Hill, 1961).

11. Stephan A. Richardson, "Organization Contrasts on British and American Ships," *Administrative Science Quarterly* (September 1956). A more detailed description of the British arrangement may be found in Peter H. Fricke, *The Social Structure of Crews* . . . (Durham, Wales: University of Wales, Department of Maritime Studies, 1974).

12. The range of ulterior motives for hiring consultants is described in a brilliant chapter on "The Advice Market" in Wilbert E. Moore, *The Conduct of the Corporation* (New York: Random House, 1962).

13. An excellent summary of IBM practices may be found in Peter F. Drucker, *Management: Tasks, Responsibility, Practices* (New York: Harper & Row, 1974), pp. 260–65.

14. Quoted by Robert E. Cole, *Work, Mobility, and Participation: A Comparative Study of American and Japanese Industry* (Berkeley: University of California Press, 1979), p. 197.

15. Edmond Cahn, *The Predicament of Democratic Man* (New York: Macmillan, 1961), pp. 178–80.

16. See the section on rumor in Gardner Lindzey and Elliot Aronson, eds., *The Handbook of Social Psychology*, 2nd ed. (Reading, Mass.: Addison-Wesley, 1969).

17. Daniel Katz, "Approaches to Managing Conflict," in Robert L. Kahan and Elise Boulding, eds., *Power and Conflict in Organizations* (New York: Basic Books, 1964).

18. David Riesman, Nathan Glazier, and Reuel Denney, *The Lonely Crowd* (Garden City, N.Y.: Doubleday Anchor Books, 1953), pp. 243–45.

19. For a general discussion of the relationship between seating arrangements and participation, see Robert Sommer, *Personal Space: The Behavioral Basis of Design* (Englewood Cliffs, N.J.: Prentice-Hall, 1969).

Chapter 3

1. David M. Ogilvy, "The Creative Chef," in G. A. Steiner, ed., *The Creative Organization* (Chicago: University of Chicago Press, 1965), p. 202.

2. Ibid., p. 203.

3. Alfred Chandler, "Strategy and Structure: The Sloan Structure at General Motors," reprinted in M. W. Meyer, ed., *Structures, Symbols and Systems* (Boston: Little, Brown, 1971).

4. Ibid., p. 354.

5. J. Patrick Wright, *On a Clear Day You Can See General Motors: John Z. De Lorean's Look Inside the Automotive Giants* (Gross Pt., Mich.: Wright Enterprises, 1979).

6. Frederick W. Hornbruch, Jr., *Raising Productivity: Ten Case Histories and Their Lessons* (New York: McGraw-Hill, 1977). For an overall systematic approach to productivity improvement see Noel M. Tichy and Jay N. Nisberg in A. Etzioni and E. W. Lehman, eds., *A Sociological Reader on Complex Organizations* (New York: Holt, Rinehart and Winston, 1980), pp. 540–59.

7. Frederick W. Taylor, "Scientific Management," reprinted in Grusky and Miller, eds., *The Sociology of Organizations: Basic Studies* (New York: Free Press, 1970), p. 49.

8. Ibid., p. 51.

9. Elton Mayo, *Human Problems of an Industrial Civilization* (New York: Macmillan, 1933); and Fritz J. Roethlisberger and William J. Dickson, *Management and the Worker* (Cambridge, Mass.: Harvard University Press, 1939).

10. Rensis Likert, *New Patterns of Management* (New York: McGraw-Hill, 1961).

11. Melville Dalton, "Managing the Managers," *Human Organization* 14, no. 3 (Fall 1955):410.

12. Joseph Bensman and Israel Gerver, "Crime and Punishment in the Factory: The Function of Deviancy in Maintaining the Social System," in J. M. Shepard, ed., *Organizational Issues in Industrial Society* (Englewood Cliffs, N.J.: Prentice-Hall, 1972), pp. 181–95.

13. For a case of pervasive cheating in a smaller organization, see Levinson and Lang, op. cit., (1981), pp. 94–95.

14. *Washington Post,* June 30, 1980.

15. Adapted from Frank Pieper, *Modular Management and Human Leadership* (Minneapolis: Methods Press, 1958), pp. 69–70.

16. Jeremy Main, "How to Battle Your Own Bureaucracy," *Fortune* (June 29, 1981), pp. 54–58. The company is Intel.

17. Robert B. Goldmann, "Work Values: Six Americans in a Swedish Plant," in D. Jones, ed., *Horizons of Industrial Productivity* (Ann Arbor: Institute of Science and Technology, University of Michigan, 1977), pp. 101–41.

18. Summarized in Bernard M. Bass and Gerald V. Barrett, *Man, Work and Organization* (Boston: Allyn & Bacon, 1972), p. 58.

19. For an interesting case history, see Dalton, "Managing the Managers," pp. 139–41.

20. Joseph S. Berliner, "A Problem in Soviet Business Administration," reprinted in Oscar Grusky and George A. Miller, eds., *The Sociology of Organizations: Basic Studies* (New York: Free Press, 1970), p. 561.

21. Peter M. Blau, *The Dynamics of Bureaucracy,* rev. ed. (Chicago: University of Chicago Press, 1963).

Chapter 4

1. Frank J. Smith, "Work Attitudes as Predictors of Attendance on a Specific Day," *Journal of Applied Psychology* 62, no. 1 (1977):16–19.

2. Roy Lewis and Rosemary Stewart, *The Managers: A New Examination of the English, German and American Executive* (New York: Mentor Books, 1961).

3. *Washington Post,* June 16, 1981, p. A16.

4. Burke D. Grandjean, "History and Career in a Bureaucratic Labor Market," *American Journal of Sociology* 86, no. 5 (March 1981):1057–92.

5. Barbara M. Korsch and Vida Francis Negrete, "Doctor-Patient Communication," *Scientific American* 227 (August 1972):66–74.

6. Sanford N. Dornbusch, "The Military Academy as an Assimilating Institution," *Social Forces* 33, no. 4 (May 1955):316–21.

7. Harry Levensen, *Organizational Diagnosis* (Cambridge, Mass.: Harvard University Press, 1972), p. 411.

8. Laurence J. Peter and Raymond Hull, *The Peter Principle* (New York: William Morrow, 1969).

9. C. H. Lawshe and A. D. McGinley, "Job performance criteria studies I. The job performance of proofreaders," *Journal of Applied Psychology* 35 (1951):316–20.

10. John C. Flanigan and Robert K. Burns, "The Employee Performance Record: A New Appraisal and Development Tool," *Harvard Business Review* 33, no. 5 (September–October 1955):95.

11. See J. Stacy Adams, "Inequity in Social Exchange," in L. Berkowitz, ed., *Advances in Experimental Social Psychology* (New York: Academic Press, 1965), pp. 265–99; and George C. Homans, *Social Behavior: Its Elementary Forms* (New York: Harcourt Brace, 1961).

12. J. Berger et al., *Distributive Justice: A Status Value Formulation,* Stanford University Technical Report no. 28 (Stanford, Calif., 1968).

13. See John M. Ivancevich and Michael E. Matteson, *Stress and Work: A Managerial Perspective* (Glenview, Illinois: Scott, Foresman, 1980).

14. For a spectacular example, see Landon Y. Jones, Jr., "Bad Days on Mount Olympus: The Big Shoot-out at the Institute for Advanced Study," *Atlantic* 233, no. 2 (February 1974):37–53.

15. Samuel A. Stouffer et al., *Studies in Social Psychology in World War II,* 4 vols. (Princeton, N.J.: Princeton University Press, 1949–50).

16. This situation, as actually observed, is described in Peter H. Fricke, *The Social Structure of Crews . . .* (Durham, Wales: University of Wales, Department of Maritime Studies, 1974).

17. Herbert A. Shepard, "Responses to Situations of Competition in Conflict," in Robert L. Cahn and Elise Boulding, *Power and Conflict in Organizations* (New York: Basic Books, 1964), pp. 130–33.

18. Orvis Collins, "Ethnic Behavior in Industry: Sponsorship and Rejection in a New England Factory," *American Journal of Sociology* 51 (January 1946):293–98.

Chapter 5

1. See Howard E. Aldrich, *Organization and Environments* (Englewood Cliffs, N.J.: Prentice-Hall, 1979), pp. 26–55.

2. For an interesting discussion of organizational stability and instability, see John W. Meyer and Brian Rowan, "Institutionalized Organizations: Formal Structure as Myth and Ceremony," in O. Grusky and G. A. Miller, *The Sociology of Organizations: Basic Studies,* second edition (New York: Free Press, 1981), pp. 530–54.

3. A full description of team management may be found in Peter H. Drucker, *Management: Tasks, Responsibilities, Practices* (New York: Harper & Row, 1974).

4. Erving Goffman, *Asylums* (New York: Anchor Books, 1961).

5. *International Herald Tribune,* October 22, 1980.

6. C. Northcote Parkinson, *Parkinson's Law and Other Studies in Administration* (Boston: Houghton-Mifflin, 1957).

7. John Freeman and Michael T. Hannan, "Growth and Decline Processes in Organizations," in D. Katz, R. Kahn and S. Adams, *The Study of Organizations* (San Francisco: Jossey-Bass, 1980), pp. 43–58.

8. See *Gains and Shortcomings in Resolving Regulatory Conflicts and Overlaps* (Washington, D.C.: U.S. General Accounting Office, PAD-81-76, June 23, 1981).

9. Theodore Caplow, *Towards Social Hope* (New York: Basic Books, 1975).

10. Conrad N. Arensberg and Arthur H. Niehoff, *Introducing Social Change: A Manual for Americans Overseas* (Chicago: Aldine, 1964), p. 77.

11. James G. March and Herman A. Simon, *Organizations* (New York: John Wiley & Sons, 1958), p. 188.

12. The original observations are somewhat inaccessible, but the film has been widely shown, and a good summary may be found in Vitus B. Droscher, *The Friendly Beast* (New York: Harper & Row, 1971), pp. 191–92.

13. Gary A. Steiner, *The Creative Organization* (Chicago: University of Chicago Press, 1965).

14. For discussion of the president's role in corporate planning, see Myles L. Mace, "The President and Corporate Planning," in Harvard Business Review, *On Management* (New York: Harper & Row, 1976), pp. 119–42.

15. Such a situation is described in detail by Neal Gross, Joseph B. Giacquinto, and Marty Bernstein, in *Implementing Organizational Innovations* (New York: Basic Books, 1971).

16. Needless to say, some of the contradictions will persist in reality whether or not they are resolved within a plan. For a despairing view of planning under those conditions, see W. Richard Scott, *Organizations: Rational, Natural and Open Systems* (Englewood Cliffs, N.J.: Prentice-Hall, 1981), pp. 270–75.

Index

Index

DATE DUE

DEC 1 8 1997			
MAR 1 4 1990			
APR 0 9 1993			